There is a land of the living and
a land of the dead
and the bridge is love
the only survival, the only meaning.

— Thornton Wilder

Blessing the Bridge

What Animals Teach Us About Death, Dying, and Beyond

RITA M. REYNOLDS

FOREWORD BY
GARY KOWALSKI

NEWSAGE PRESS
TROUTDALE, OREGON

BLESSING THE BRIDGE: WHAT ANIMALS TEACH US ABOUT
DEATH, DYING, AND BEYOND
Copyright © 2001 by Rita M. Reynolds
Paperback Original ISBN 0-939165-38-4

NewSage Press
PO Box 607
Troutdale, OR 97060-0607
503-695-2211

web site: www.newsagepress.com
email: info@newsagepress.com

Cover Design by George Foster
Book Design by Patricia Keelin
Cover Photo is Zach, photographed by Lucy Aron.

Printed in the United States on recycled paper with soy ink.

Distributed in the United States and Canada by
Publishers Group West 800-788-3123 (U.S.)
Publishers Group West 416-934-9900 (Canada)

Library of Congress Cataloging-in-Publication Data

Reynolds, Rita M., 1947-
    Blessing the bridge : what animals teach us about death, dying,
    and beyond / by Rita M. Reynolds.
        p. cm.
    Includes bibliographical references (p.).
    ISBN 0-939165-38-4 (pbk.)
        1. Pet owners–Psychology. 2. Pets–Death–Psychological aspects. 3.
    Bereavement–Psychological aspects. I. Title.

SF411.47 .R48 2000
155.9'37–dc21   00-035124

2 3 4 5 6 7 8 9

For Oliver, the bravest of dogs,
and for all the animals, humans, and beings of light,
here and beyond, who grace my life.

Acknowledgments

Throughout my life, so many beings have guided, taught, encouraged, loved, and inspired me. They have helped me form who I am today, and the direction I, and my work, will take tomorrow. In all the crises you have been there. In the sad times you have lifted me, and in the uncertain times, you have helped ground me.

The beings of light, my beloved angelic guides, thank you for standing by my side with your boundless love and gentle wisdom.

My mother, Frances Chandler Morris, who encouraged my love of nature. Thank you for your wisdom and love, on my side of life, and from the other side now.

The animals, every one of them, from ladybugs and spiders to cows and donkeys: Thank you for teaching me the important things in life—courage, loyalty, unconditional love, living in the moment, appreciation for the so-called ordinary things, joy, peace. My deepest gratitude to those animals who have shared their living, and their dying with me; Hannah, Emily, Angelo, Twigger, Oliver, Christina, Nori, Miso, and Julia, Robyn, Bart and Susan, Stella, and Easter—to name a few.

Many thanks to my family, who has exhibited extreme patience, understanding and support for my unusual line of work: My husband, Doug, our sons, Michael and Tim, my "adopted daughter," Jo, my favorite sister, Sylvia (Tao), and Roger F. Duncan and Mary C. Duncan.

Infinite gratitude to Robert Partridge, D.V.M. and all my friends at The Animal Hospital of Waynesboro. And to Dan Woodworth, D.V.M. for taking care of my large (farm) animals. Your skill and compassionate approach to veterinary medicine have made my work with animals possible.

To the outstanding healers, teachers, and friends who have been so much a process of this book, and who share my vision of reverence for all life, including: Mary K. Birkholz, Eleanor Cox Sojka, Dr. Nick Sojka, Ellen T. Powe, Gabe and Polly Swift, Marilyn Preston Evans, Frederick Evans, Bernie Siegel, M.D., Stewart Metz, M.D., Patti and Kevin Cole, Joan Brundage, Mary Beth Artz, Deborah Straw, Sally Rosenthal, Susan Chernak McElroy, Sharon Callahan, Sue Jenkinson, Sharon Osborne, T.J. Banks, Marissa Spooner, Elaine Abicca, Sandy Carlson, Maureen Cussons, Pat Daly-Lipe, Harriet Mann, Judith Minter, Joan Martin, Gary Kowalski, Joanne Lauck, Marianne Meretz, Annette Overstreet, Nancy Eismann, Bud and Beverly Eismann, Ruth Dalsky, Lorenza Piper, Mary Ranson, Shirley Roberts, Dr. Ellen K. Rudolph, Anne Guerrant, Meda Hill, Dr. Christine Rosner, Lois Schneider, Dug Steele, Rev. Mother Ambrose, Billie Wilson, Rebecca Maloney, Steve and Jane Mullins, Carol Beasley, Jeanne, Charlie, and Christine Houser, Edna Gillespie, Bill and Tina Hodge, Shirley Anne Briggs, Harriet Mann, and LaVina Staab, Frema Rauh, Elizabeth Hunton, and Nancy Palmero. For those whose names I have inadvertently omitted, please know how much I appreciate you as well.

To Maureen Michelson, my patient editor and publisher at NewSage Press: Thank you for your vision regarding the importance and sanctity of animals, and for your willingness and hard work to bring my vision regarding animals, to the public.

And finally, to Eleanor K. Friede, who was the first person to see the value in my manuscript, and to Barbara Bowen, my outstanding agent, guide, and good friend.

Contents

Foreword

Lately, I have been thinking about the last words of that great American preacher of the 19th century, Henry Ward Beecher. As he lay upon his deathbed, he uttered, *And now, the mystery!*

Imagine meeting the end of life, not with anxiety or dread, but with curiosity and anticipation. Beecher's brief remark reveals wisdom, hope and courage. These were the parting words of a man who had long reflected on matters of life and death and, without knowing all the answers, made his peace with eternity.

I find that same sense of equanimity, fortitude, and quiet faith contained in the volume you now hold within your hands. *Blessing the Bridge* by Rita Reynolds is in turn heartwarming and thought-provoking, but always marked by an unshakeable assurance that the end of life can be faced without fear. She has learned that animals, who always seem to live closest to the marrow of existence, can teach us to accept death as an opening for love and wonder.

There is no doubt that Rita, who has helped so many creatures make the passage from this world to the next, has a gift for this work. Healing the sick, tending to the dying, and comforting the bereaved and brokenhearted are no easy tasks, and none but the pure of spirit are called to such a difficult vocation. I think of exceptional individuals such as Mother Teresa, who spent her life caring for the forsaken and dying of Calcutta, or the poet Walt Whitman, who comforted wounded soldiers as a volunteer nurse in hospitals during the Civil War. Although she is less famous, Rita Reynolds is no less compassionate in her commitment to care for the forgotten and neglected. Others might look upon the assortment of dogs and ducks and donkeys who come to her farm as mere castaways or strays, but for Rita, each one is an expression of the Infinite. And however diseased or disabled, each one is precious and beloved.

Rita's special mission is to make sure that each of these creatures is accompanied across the final threshold with a gentle hand and a calming presence. Rita's own life reminds me of Mother Teresa's dictum that, "There are no great deeds, only small deeds, done with great love." And Rita's confidence that a better life awaits us beyond the great unknown recalls Whitman's comment "To die is different from what anyone supposes, and luckier." Like the saints and poets, Rita Reynolds has learned to look upon the world, not only with the eyes, but with the heart.

Naturally, she has developed her own philosophy, drawn from many sources, to guide her on her chosen path. Some of her ideas, like the Buddhist teachings she introduces, are familiar friends that I find helpful in my personal practice. Other beliefs, like Rita's reliance on angels, are not part of my own experience. Yet I am certain that if angels do exist, they must look and act very much like Rita Reynolds. How fortunate the animals are who have her near in their hour of need!

What then is the essence of Rita's message? On the south portal of a mosque in India there is an old inscription:

Jesus, on whom be peace, has said: The world is a bridge, go over it, but do not install yourselves on it.

Rita Reynolds reminds us of the lesson that other great teachers have also imparted. Life is a bridge, from the miracle of birth to the mystery of death — from time to what is timeless. With the help of books like this one, we can better appreciate the blessings of joy and companionship to be discovered along the way.

— The Reverend Gary Kowalski
Author, *The Souls of Animals* and
Goodbye Friend: Healing Wisdom for Anyone Who Has Ever Lost a Pet

Blessing the Bridge

ONE

Creating a Sanctuary

In the midst of a routine day I gathered my dog, Oliver, into my arms, and held his soft, small body close to mine "There is a strong possibility," I explained, "that the cancer growing inside you will eventually cause us to be separated from each other." As the word "separated" left my mouth, his face rose to mine. Although blind, his eyes danced, shining with life. I sensed that he was seeing on another level, within and through me. "You will change worlds and I will have to remain behind, but I will always love you." Oliver turned his head downward as my words and tears cascaded over him. A knowing flowed between Oliver and me that in truth we could never be separated, and that everything was perfect, even the cancer.

But I had not always felt so. When I had heard the diagnosis three months earlier, I had immediately made Oliver's cancer an enemy. That cancer was the monster that would tear my dear friend of eight years away from me. Later, in a reflective moment I realized that by declaring war on the cancer, I was making all of Oliver's cells — the whole basic structure of his body — my enemy as well. From that moment, rather than cursing his cells, I began loving and blessing them, even the cancerous ones, hoping this approach would cure him.

But what if he died anyway? I asked myself in doubtful moments. *Would I have accomplished anything at all, or wasted energy, time, and emotion? Was I entrapping myself in false hope, blind faith, and utter stupidity?* I wondered if I was setting myself up for a hard and terrible disappointment.

Oliver's tumor was in his bladder. The medical prognosis was that the cancer would not respond to surgery, chemotherapy, or radiation. After introspection and prayer, I decided to begin my own integrative therapy for Oliver. My intuition, always my best guide, directed me to use sound and music therapy, color and light, supportive nutrition, and the prayer support of friends and family. At the same time, I also realized that it might just be Oliver's time to go.

As we proceeded with these alternative healing methods, I began to realize that everything I was doing for Oliver was appropriate for possibly curing his physical condition, while at the same time helping him through his dying if that would be the outcome. I was no longer attempting a "cure-or-nothing approach," which would imply success versus failure or winning versus losing. I had ended my battle against the cancer.

No longer was this therapy focused on my little dog alone. Now, Oliver and I were moving in tandem through a mutual and inter-supportive healing on infinite levels. As with so many of the animals who had been in my care, I was once again learning when and how to let Oliver go, making sure I did so with unconditional love, grace, and peace.

We walked through our healing, step by step. Nothing long range. I felt compelled to give up all my goals, including healing him. My job was simply to offer Oliver my full participation and accept each moment as perfect, no matter what was going on. It was easier for Oliver, he had no expectations. But I also knew Oliver and I were not alone. There was a boundless, pure spirit that led us with love. Oliver shone with that love.

But when finally faced with the certainty of Oliver's impending death, I once again struggled with my emotional attachment and inevitable sense of failure. I questioned everything. Was the pain I saw cross his face only momentary? Would it pass, and then we would still have more time together? Or was it his way of asking for compassionate release? I could not decide, so I turned within and prayed for help. The guidance came and I knew Oliver was ready to leave.

The day before Oliver died, he laid his head on my foot as I wrote down my thoughts about him. He communicated to me, *Don't begin missing me yet. Share this moment with me, everything is as it is meant to be. And if you let me, I will guide you for all the moments to come.*

"I will," I responded, out loud, knowing he was pleased. And so Oliver's life on Earth ended well.

My friend and teacher joined me in this lifetime as a honey-colored terrier named Oliver. Through his living and dying, he taught me there is no such thing as life versus death, or success versus failure. Love given and received, moment by moment, is all that really matters.

Since childhood I have been offered countless opportunities to understand the essence of death, and despite the pain and suffering that seem to accompany it, to realize its luminescence. I have learned over the past four and a half decades that the animals come to teach me, among other things, a new understanding of the dying process from which so many of us uncomfortably turn away.

Animals are masters in their own manner of the flow of birth, growth, death, and beyond. They continue to impress upon me the importance of preparing — not out of fear, but out of wonderment — for one of the most important events in every life: death. The animals have taught me ways to approach death and dying that can enrich and enlighten.

I haven't always thought that to be true. I've done my share of cursing and fighting death, of begging my creature friends not to die, of wrestling with "Why this one, why now...?" My preference would be for everyone to live forever, provided they are in good spirits and excellent health. Few people will hear me state that the death of a friend, human or animal, is easy or immediately enlightening when I am in the thick of it. Honestly speaking, I dread losing my companions. Loss hurts, it is exhausting, and while I do always grow spiritually, emotionally, and mentally with each passing, I never look forward to another's death with joy and anticipation.

"May you live to at least forty," I tell each of the animals who come into my care. "May my children inherit you," I whisper into the long, soft brown ears of my three donkeys who have a long life span and may out live me. I'm not ashamed of this attitude. I would be more ashamed if I denied my vulnerability. It is my vulnerability that keeps me open to the suffering and pain of others, which in turn, stirs within me the compassion and loving kindness that always are the best healers.

Over time I continue to learn how to be fully open and willing to take on the suffering of others in order to return support, love, and compassion to them. I often spend years in a powerful, loving relationship with a creature and allow myself to become hopelessly attached. But I am willing to learn through the shattering times as well as the exquisite times. I've stood by my animal friends while they've experienced all manner of passing, from peaceful to painful, from too quick to agonizingly slow. But for all my complaints, I hold them, love them, and try to pay attention as they die.

Frequently, my journey to a more expansive understanding of dying has been rough, the learning difficult, the sense of loss enormous. My own resistance and past conditioning have been stubborn. But still my beloved teachers come: finned and furred, shelled and scaled, two- and four-legged, and no doubt some back for second and third attempts to enlighten me. It's worth their effort, the animals assure me, and it's definitely worth mine. Repeatedly, the animals have shown me death from different angles and perspectives. They've led me to face my own fears of mortality and move past them by demonstrating their own immortality. The animals' teachings guide me through my life's work of helping those who are dying, and to comfort those who must say goodbye and remain behind.

⌐

It is impossible to open one's doors, literally and figuratively, to creatures and avoid the trauma of their illnesses, dying, and death. My passion for helping injured, abandoned, and abused animals began early, probably the moment I was able to crawl after bugs. Bugs were my first friends and there always seemed to be plenty of them in need of rescuing. To this day I help spiders and hornets out of the house and check water buckets in the donkey and goat barn to invariably find one (or more) unfortunate creature struggling for his life. From bumblebees to tiny beetles I lift them to safety, sending them along the fence rail, never doubting that their existence is as precious as any other being on this planet.

Ever since I was a child, when given a choice of footwear, I wore moccasins. It was instinctual for me, as was lying in the grass for hours, watching the miniature world of insects and bugs, or climbing a tree as high as I dared and conversing with birds and squirrels. Moccasins, still my favorite shoe, close the distance between myself and Earth. With moccasins I can step lightly, silently, and reverently. They allow me to make every step a gentle, respectful one. Boots, even sneakers, clump and crash across the ground, crushing in wide swaths plants and animals who make their homes and paths there.

Even when I stumbled perilously through adolescence and early adulthood I kept my great love for Earth and all her nonhuman beings. I found I related more easily to animals, trees, wind, and stones than to others of my own species. Always, they have all been part of the "group" I call my family.

Dogs and cats in increasing numbers came later when in 1978, married with two young sons of my own, we moved from New

England to the small farm in the foothills of the Virginia Blue Ridge Mountains where we still live today. We already had two dogs and two cats when we arrived at the farm, only to find an unwanted beagle on the doorstep of our new home. From there it didn't take long for that invisible sign to "appear" at the end of the farm drive that apparently said, *Vacancy. Wounded, starving, orphaned or abandoned? Apply within. All applicants accepted.* Eventually, I formally named our farm-turned-sanctuary "Howling Success."

I established one rule early on. Whatever creature in need appears here, stays for life; no one is turned away. And by some magical accounting, no more animals have arrived than could be well cared for at one time. Yet, hardly has one died than another suddenly arrives on the front lawn. Or an animal becomes known to me through someone in such a way that there is no doubt the animal should be with me at the sanctuary.

Along with dogs and cats come the more unusual ones. There have been a variety of goats, including Marigold, rescued from death because she only produced buck (male) kids. There were six stray domestic ducks who wandered into the backyard one evening; the black-and-white spotted rooster, Cezanne, who fled from a neighbor's yard (he was destined for soup) to hide among our hens. Cezanne died of old age ten years later. A partial list at best, that also includes Betsy and Bob, the two orphaned newborn field mice I found in a hundred pound sack of grain; a one-eyed hen named Robyn; three shaggy donkeys, and an ancient box turtle named Henry who lived in our rose garden.

Our sons, Michael and Tim, loved each new addition to our family and helped tend to the creatures with only mild complaint. They learned invaluable lessons in caring for other living beings through life and through death. My husband, Doug, however, not quite the animal enthusiast I have always been, tolerated the on-rolling influx of needy animals with useless protests that got lost in the uproar of barks and brays, quacks, and baas. Still, he has, without exception, been a strong and caring supporter, and none of my work with the animals would have been as successful without the close and caring nature of Doug, Michael, and Tim. But to be fair, originally the chickens were Doug's idea. The first afternoon in our new home, the previous owner, Lennie, asked if we wanted to keep the twenty-two hens and one large rooster he had raised there. New to Virginia and to farming I said, "No," at the precise moment, Doug, raised on a farm, said, "Yes." The chickens stayed and I've taken care of them since, never regretting a moment with them.

Despite such initial hesitancy on my part at times, (rare though it has been) each animal has quickly taken its place on the farm, seemingly of his or her own accord. As if with a mind of its own, this small sanctuary has from the beginning evolved almost by some pre-ordained plan with purpose, direction, and certainly adventure. The animals who come here always enrich my life with a new perspective on caregiving. I have learned when to press on in the support of the process of life and health, and eventually, inevitably, when to let go and support the dying process.

～

Over the past fifteen years of working with animals I have learned how to allow a dying creature's passage to unfold as naturally as possible without the interference of confusion, fear, or regret on my part. Fifteen years ago, however, I was far less prepared when Domino died. But it was the day Domino died that I began my own journey — in a most unexpected way — into conscious dying work with animals and their families.

Domino was my mother's dog and his death from leukemia had been both shocking and painful for everyone. While my mother appeared to cope, I sensed in her a grief too deeply tied to a lifetime of loneliness and abuse to be fully resolved. And there was my mother's fear of her own mortality and the vast uncertain mystery that stretches beyond the last breath. I, too, had great difficulty facing the situation. I had too little spiritually to offer my mother in order that we might both understand and successfully work through Domino's dying. I believe this hurt me more than Domino's actual death.

That afternoon when Domino died, we placed his body in the back of our car and drove over Afton Mountain to the veterinary hospital for cremation. Nothing much was said until I suggested we stop at a restaurant at the top of the mountain on the return trip. The view across the Shenandoah Valley to the west and Albemarle County to the east always seemed to lift our spirits. Over lunch my mother reminisced about her beloved companion and I, barely nibbling my sandwich, tried to listen politely. My mind, however, seemed to be pulled elsewhere, as if into a void, beyond my control.

Suddenly, there was what I have come to accept as a knowing — my intuition perhaps, or an unseen angelic guide? Both were supportive "friends" familiar to me since childhood and I was not surprised to receive a brief yet complete message. The message seemed to be absolutely appropriate while at the same time distressing. However, the message was clear: The work I was supposed to do for the rest of my life involved helping animals through the dying process and assisting humans in understanding the true nature and luminescence of dying and life beyond. I would provide a hospice for animals and their human families — a novel idea at least. From the message, I surmised that much of my work would be with elder animals. Then the void dissolved without further explanation.

I have always honored my intuition or from wherever or whomever such guidance comes, yet this time I balked. Here it was, probably my great purpose in life, but I questioned how could I possibly help others with their dying, and be there for families with their grief when I cried over dying butterflies? Silently I announced to the mysterious messenger that I would prefer any other kind of work with animals and their human families, but not this. In my mind the matter was closed. We do, after all, have free will. This being the case, I said nothing of the message, or my thoughts regarding it, to anyone else.

My animal care work continued, tending to those who found our sanctuary, sometimes by twos now. With Michael and Tim both in elementary school, I began writing articles about my animal-related experiences, striving continually for public awareness of the sanctity of all life, an issue that has been precious to me since early childhood. However, in my writings, in my day-to-day interaction with "our" animals, I continued to stubbornly ignore, avoid, or otherwise cringe from the less-than-pleasant aspects of illness and death.

A sense of infinite compassion and unconditional love have always been a part of me. My life's work is to relieve suffering wherever I encounter it. Albert Schweitzer's ethic of Reverence For Life, but especially animals, plants, and trees is and has been my personal philosophy since I was five when my grandmother first began reading his books to me. And there was that rule about not turning anyone away. So quite naturally, and with increasing frequency, I began to find myself assisting both elderly and dying animals, as well as responding to the pain and grief people feel when losing their animal companions.

As the years passed and the opportunities arose, I was amazed at how easily I accepted the work. Step by step, as if in some structured university/universal program, I began to understand the process of death in new terms and constructively began to practice what I had learned.

Still, I had not connected with the idea that the animals were the teachers and I was the student. I did not realize this had been unfolding for many years until a most remarkable presence entered my life. In May 1994 my veterinarian, Dr. Robert Partridge, asked if I could help find a loving home for his parents' thirteen-year-old golden retriever, Penny Partridge. Both in their eighties, Mr. and Mrs. Partridge had a difficult time caring for Penny. Giving her up was extremely painful for them, but their selfless love made them look to her best interests. Throughout the summer I tried to find Penny a good home, but no one wanted such an old dog. They didn't want her "dying on them."

In August, Dr. Partridge asked me again, this time with a definite note of anxiety in his voice. His father wanted Penny euthanized, he said, if no home could be found. Yet Penny was still amazingly spry and healthy for her age and size. Again I offered to continue the search, apologizing for not taking her in myself. Our house was already bursting with thirteen resident dogs.

Late that August I sat on the front porch swing, sipping a fresh cup of coffee and enjoying the early morning sun rising from the mountains and fields around our home. Once again I felt myself drift into that void — a place filled with peace and light, a comfortable and familiar place I trusted completely. And there, streaming through my consciousness came that knowing, this time thrilling in its perfection and appropriateness: *Penny was to come here to live out the rest of her life*. Somehow I felt this was all part of a magnificent plan; the synchronicity was perfect, the full purpose yet to be revealed. This time not only did I listen carefully, I agreed without hesitation, in fact with expectation and joy.

Penny arrived three weeks later with a contented sense of already belonging. During her stay with us she reminded me of many excellent qualities of life I had temporarily forgotten. She faced change with a sense of adventure, and she taught me the importance of playfulness no matter what one's age or creaky bones. During her time in our home, and later, in her passing, Penny demonstrated how to bring people together in a loving manner. Strength and courage were qualities she displayed daily, as did all the other animals around me, both wild and domesticated. Yet in Penny, they were qualities that seemed to shine. For the first time in her life she learned how to manage stairs. She discovered cats and found them fascinating to watch, to wash, and to chase. And she learned about pecking order, alpha dogs, packs — all new to one who once had been an only dog.

Penny had been with us only six months, yet there was a familiarity about her as if she had lived with me forever. I felt as if some ancient sage dwelled in that massive golden frame. Then one evening without warning she simply collapsed. In subsequent days we discovered she had developed inoperable cancer that would become increasingly painful. She was euthanized by the gentle hand of Dr. Partridge.

Penny's death at the age of fourteen offered me new experiences and insights into the passage from life. For example, Dr. Partridge phoned with the news of finding her cancer, immediately following the exploratory surgery. Together we agreed it would be kindest to Penny to simply not let her wake up from the anesthesia. This meant, however, that I would not be present at her death. And initially, this was difficult for me. I did not want Penny to feel I had abandoned her. Yet, as I sat in prayer, I felt strongly that she understood my physical absence at such an important time. And in some inexplicable way, Penny assured me that on our soul level, we were not apart from one another at all.

In moving through my own grieving process over Penny's death, I followed the steps I had offered to others so many times in the past few years. I sat in silence and sent loving, supportive messages to Penny. Then I spoke aloud to her, sensing that wherever she was, she would hear and appreciate my words. In meditation I visualized our minds and hearts joining. I allowed myself to continue to cry as needed, sometimes in the middle of the night, often as I set out dinner bowls for the other dogs, hers painfully absent. I washed and put away Penny's favorite blanket, to be used for the next animal in need. I wrote a lengthy letter to Dr. Partridge, his family, and the hospital staff who had gathered over the months to assist her transition from her previous home to mine, and from mine to the beyond. I detailed all she had reminded me of, new things she had taught me, and the ways I would continue to honor her presence in the universe.

I realized I could, after all, keep an open door and heart to other elder animals in need of love and assistance in their final days on

Earth. I could be a gentle "embrace" that eased their journey through dying. Finally, a few days after Penny's death, I stood in the middle of my living room surrounded by thirteen eager canines and eight pensive felines, and declared these intentions to Penny Partridge, and all of Life everywhere.

Since Penny's passing I have often felt her spirit close by, almost as if I could see her, but not quite. The guidance I received after Domino's death seemed to be the same "voice" or energy that led Penny and me to each other. The bond Penny and I formed inspires me to continue the work in her memory.

Penny Partridge left me with a new awareness about life and death. And now, each creature, in his or her own way, continues to broaden that awareness. No two experiences are ever the same. Sometimes I am overwhelmed by the waves of beauty inherent in the process of death. At other times, I only get a glimpse of that beauty. Each new encounter with an animal's passing requires that I have enough humility to recognize and accept all that I still don't know. Then and only then am I able to firmly integrate their teaching into my heart and be ready to pass it along to the next one, human or creature who, through her suffering, calls me still deeper into my own evolution.

⌣

There is no question in my mind that angelic guides play an important role in my work with animals. It is my understanding that beings of light, whom I refer to as angelic guides, are with all living beings. There is no one who does not have an angel to guide and protect him or her. In Sanskrit, these remarkable beings are called *devas*, or Shining Ones. Some mystics consider them to be aspects of God, or The Beloved. However one wishes to refer to them, there are two considerations of these beings of light that are worth noting. My first observation is that while it is their great joy and self-appointed task to assist those of us struggling on the physical plane, unless circum-stances are extraordinary (and I haven't a clue how they decide this), these angelic beings will not step in and help unless we ask them to. To do so would be considered interference in one's free will and an inap-propriate manipulation of karma, that process by which everything is balanced. We must be responsible for our choices regarding how we move through an experience, so that we may evolve unhindered through our growing awareness of our true nature.

The other quality I attribute to these guides is complete, unequivocal, non-judgmental love. They exemplify true compassion that does not discriminate.

Often, I speak to these angelic beings in prayer, whether I am desperate over something or someone, or if I just express appreciation for their loyalty, love, encouragement, and protection. When I am centered enough to clearly hear my guides, I always receive remarkable insight and wisdom. They give me straightforward common sense that is perfect for the situation for which I am inquiring. Without judgment or intrusion they, and all they teach, are the epitome of sacred love and compassion.

Conversing with one's guides is simple, safe, and profound, and available to everyone. I cannot stress this enough; call on them. These guides are "here" and you will know it.

But the beings of light offer a service even beyond that of helping us when we call on them. Much like the physician or midwife who helps mother and infant through the birthing process, the angelic ones stand ready to assist those who are dying, but from the other side, so to speak, waiting on the spirit-side of the bridge called death. They are ready to guide, encourage, and protect those who are traveling out of physical existence.

Angels and animals continue to stream through my life experiences, calling for my loving attention to the details of life *and* death. I have learned that believing in this unseen presence requires that I must have faith in those processes that are far beyond my limited comprehension.

Increasingly, I am able to open up and embrace what I consider to be a cosmic consciousness that knows no beginning and no end.

My years of working with animals have shown me that life is not limited to the physical existence, bound by birth and death of the body, but extends infinitely. The animals teach me greater spiritual awareness and acceptance. Even through my most challenging stages of growth, when I have been blinded and motivated by fear, anger, impatience, and despair, my belief in life beyond death sustains me.

And all of that being said, I still struggle against the death of a beloved friend, no longer from fear of death and the unknown, but only from my own sense of loss. Eventually, I return to my inner knowing and remember that my friend is merely continuing his or her journey in spirit form. Our relationship, which cannot be terminated by death, is only a temporary separation. Trusting this inner knowing, I once again find my balance and happily continue the work.

So when I question *why* I am doing this work with sick and dying animals, the answers come — from Domino and Oliver, from a baby bird and four very old goats, and of course, from a beautiful dog named Penny Partridge. So many animals have shaken my confusion over questions about life and death, quieted my exhausted mind, and continue to help me find my way.

Two

Each Creature Brings a Gift

Can death really be beautiful? I never used to think so. When animals died at my sanctuary I would grit my teeth and somehow get through the process staying close by their side. But after a while, I began to realize that even the most difficult deaths left me with a gift, and insight — or maybe just a moment when something beautiful occurred.

In the beginning, I didn't recognize the gift at all. Eventually, I would find it in retrospect when mulling through memories of my beloved creature friends. In most recent years, I've come to know the gift the second it occurs no matter how exhausted I am, no matter the extent of my grief. Now it is almost as if I am two people, one observing and the other reacting to the same situation.

In 1971, the first dog Doug and I adopted, was a black-and-tan, mixed-breed dog we named Penny, long before Penny Partridge, entered our lives. This first dog showed me the beautiful side of dying. By the time Penny was eight years old, she had moved three times with us across five states, witnessed the addition of two children to the family as well as many other dogs, cats, chickens, and goats. Always, Penny patiently endured her human companions' difficult spiritual and emotional adjustments as we continued that painful process of maturing. She never failed to stand by us, and guard and greet us as if we were the most special people in the world.

When in the spring of that eighth year she developed systemic lupus erythematosus, we all felt compelled to help her recover as best we could. But because the study of this illness in dogs was new at the time, we were unaware that lupus is irreversible and degenerative. For four long months, while we tried every treatment available, Penny continually struggled and in her final month of life developed a massive malignant tumor on her left lung. Her breathing became so labored that taking even a few steps was difficult. In order to make our daily visit to her favorite place in the woods, Doug and I would take turns carrying her.

The September morning of her death bore a brilliant sun and cloudless blue sky that had opened up between two days of cold rain. By six in the morning it was apparent that Penny was near death. I called the animal hospital, but Dr. Partridge had not come in yet. While obviously in some discomfort, I felt Penny wouldn't suffer long and I was sure she would prefer to die at home with the family she loved so much.

I carried Penny to the front porch, and sitting on the sun-filled floor with her, held her head in my lap. Only her continued gasping for air indicated any life remained and she appeared unaware of me or our surroundings. I wondered if her soul had already left the body when she stiffened her legs and released a moan that seemed to come from a bottomless cavern.

At that moment my eye caught the dark shape of our fifteen-year old black cat, Thomas, moving silently from the living room to the table beside me. He crouched there, keen yellow eyes studying human and dog below him. I strongly sensed that he knew precisely what was happening. His presence was a relief, supporting me as a friend and encouraging Penny in her transition work.

Thomas never moved from his spot. Usually, he would eat early while I made coffee, then immediately set off for a day of hunting and exploring. This particular Saturday was the only time in his seventeen years with us that Thomas stayed at home so late into the day.

Within twenty minutes from the time I brought Penny to the porch, her entire body appeared to change, to become lighter, and softer. Her eyes closed and her mouth, no longer gaping to pull in air, closed quietly as well without any signs of resistance. As I continued to hold her close to me, she seemed to move into a second stage of dying, a transition I now have learned to recognize as probably the moment of the soul's withdrawal.

Her body continued to soften in my hands and as it did, her breathing relaxed, eased on into stillness. So beautiful did her face become, her bare whispering of breath, effortless. I began to weep, not from grief but joy — the sort of releasing joy that comes from a magnificent piece of music, or from the gentle touch of an understanding friend. Penny never experienced "death throes" nor did she show any signs of pain as she withdrew from life. She simply bowed out of life with all the grace of a dancer.

Thomas and I remained with Penny for nearly an hour after her death as the last warmth of life slipped from her body. Then the inevitable cleansing waves of grief rose up as I began to miss her. Thomas watched, his wise, silent cat presence communicating with no apparent concern. It was as if he had seen her step from life to light and saw little difference between the two conditions. At the end of the hour Thomas stretched, washed his paws and whiskers, and left to begin his day, satisfied that his friend Penny was safely on her way.

⌒

Gratitude, when sincerely and clearly communicated, is one of the finest gifts that can be given or received. My goat, Josephine, was the bearer of this gift upon her death. She was one of the youngest of our goat herd, although she had attained the respectable age of thirteen.

She was such a pretty goat. A splash of her mother's Swiss Alpine breed gave her gorgeous markings of wide black and gold bands. She was mostly of the Nubian breed and sported "airplane ears" — not-quite long and low-hanging, typical of her father's Nubian side, yet not-quite short. They pointed straight upward, influenced by her mother's Alpine side. Josephine's ears just sort of bounced half way in between when she walked, adding a comical look to her beautiful face and enchanting Mona Lisa smile for which goats are so famous.

We had just lost one of our other goats, Andrew, unexpectedly, probably to heart failure, according to our large-animal veterinarian, Dr. Dan Woodworth. (We call him Dr. Dan in order to differentiate between three generations of Dr. Woodworths at the same hospital!) Three days later, while the remainder of the herd was out grazing, I thought I saw Josephine, whom I affectionately called Josie, stagger slightly. I couldn't be sure, almost as if I sensed it intuitively before I actually looked at her. But as much as I studied Josie and all the goats that afternoon, there was no more staggering by anyone. She ate dinner and seemed content. I began to relax until Doug, who had been moving hay, came around the front of the barn. "Something's wrong with that goat," he said, pointing at Josie. "I don't think she's feeling too well." In that moment my peace of mind fled.

The next day Josie ate well, but definitely staggered. By that evening she staggered noticeably, leaned against the barn wall as if exhausted, and ate less. The next morning I took her to the animal hospital for blood profiles and other tests. The prognosis was guarded: perhaps a lack of potassium, most likely lymph cancer, which Dr. Dan said was the most common cause of death in older goats and sheep.

Again, we entered the agonizing cycle of trying to find the problem, its causes and cure. Was it a dietary deficiency or cancer? Her lymph nodes appeared to be normal. I spent day and night in the barn, trying to cover all the bases, yet I had the dreadful inner feeling that we were losing the battle. It's times like this that I consider the merciful release of euthanasia, which can be a hard call to make.

After four days I knew Josie was not only in great pain, but that she would not recover. Four days had seemed like a decade. I was exhausted, depressed, unable to lose that sense of failure that tends to creep insidiously upon those of us who dare to care fully for others despite the outcome. But it was time. There I was loading up a goat into the back of my car, talking to her, and talking to God all the way over Afton Mountain. I asked for peace for Josie and myself, and asked for courage, strength, and a quiet release.

Josie may have heard me, but I don't think so; her pain kept her close inside of herself, her head turned down in weakness, her eyes vacant and distracted. At the animal hospital, Dr. Dan showed me by moving his hand rapidly in front of her frantically blinking eyes, how her brain was reacting in spasms, probably due to excessive pain. We lifted Josie out of the car and carefully laid her on the ground, her head turned away from me. I spoke softly to her, placed my hand along her back, and told her it was okay to let go. I told her she was going to a great place, I'd probably see her again, and in just a few minutes all the pain would be gone.

As Dr. Dan inserted the needle into her neck a remarkable thing occurred. In the five or so seconds before the medicine took effect, Josie raised her head off the ground, turned her face toward me, and locked eyes with mine. Her gaze was penetrating, steady, and calm. It was an unmistakable communication. Then she was gone. Being somewhat weary by this point, my first reaction was negative, afraid she was wondering why I was doing this to her. But an autopsy later that day revealed her chest area to be filled with malignant tumors. Now I know she was simply saying, "Thank you."

Such gifts come as well from the briefest of encounters with wild creatures who are dying. I have learned to pay close and compassionate attention to each one, even to the minutest insect taking its final breath. Some simply die without apparent struggle, as if they instinctively know that leaving their body is the most natural thing in the world. And I watch them move through their process with awe. But with other creatures, when struggling is apparent, I feel compelled to step in and ease their way. It can be a lonely, discouraging time for me unless I am mindful of each moment, see beyond the struggle, and stay aware of the inevitable gift, as in the following account.

Two baby birds, their eyes swollen shut, lay too still beneath the maple tree by the back door. Having apparently fallen from their nest, one was already dead. The other was too severely injured to live much longer, but when I lifted her carefully into my hand she opened her tiny mouth for food and reached upward towards the warmth of my face. There was no evidence of either parent or nest. While I cradled this wavering life in my hand, I felt her abandonment, her aloneness, and my heart ached. My immediate impulse was to relieve her suffering and the gentlest way I could think of was suffocation. Gently placing the bird back under the tree, I went to find a cloth but I didn't get far. Everything inside of me cried, "No!" and I sensed beyond doubt that although the bird appeared to be suffering, I could not take responsibility for ending this particular life. I have resorted to euthanasia for other animals over the years, always through a veterinarian, however, for this one I could not.

What now? I could only focus on the little bird, her heart beating against my palm. Buttercups came to mind, the small field of wild blooms behind the barn. I would lay the bird there and call on my angelic friends to ease her on her journey. Feeling tremendous grief, I carried the small bird around the barn.

As I walked toward the field of buttercups, I was astonished to see right in the midst of them, tall and vibrant, an enormous plant of wild mustard in full bloom. This in itself would not be extraordinary except that other wild mustard plants, so plentiful in fields and along roadways in April and May, had gone to seed weeks ago. Laying the nestling beneath the flowers, I asked her forgiveness if I was making an inappropriate decision and I offered a prayer and blessing for a peaceful release. I also thanked the wild mustard plant and who or whatever else might be motivating such compassion. Within a very short time, the little bird sighed softly and died without struggle.

How perfectly everything in this remarkable event came together to assist the gentle release of a soul from her body. This tiny creature, through her dying, reminded me that the Mystery, the power of Spirit, is always present everywhere, in everyone — in a nestling, a plant, myself.

THREE

Euthanasia:
The Merciful Release

I really didn't want to answer the phone. I had set aside a few precious hours to work on my writing and there were deadlines to consider. But people know I work with animals, and often call for advice or support. By the fourth ring, when the answering machine had not picked up the call, I knew I should answer.

The almost imperceptible catch in the soft voice on the other end of the line instantly alerted me to the urgency of the caller.

"Is this Rita Reynolds?" the person asked tentatively. This is Sue Brown. You don't know me, but — oh, is this a good time to call?"

"Yes," I heard myself reply, "it's a perfect time. How may I help you?"

No phone call I receive is like another, nor are one person's needs and concerns similar to another person's. What was familiar in Sue Brown's voice was the agony that permeated every cautiously offered word, and the obvious intense effort to hold back tears.

"I hope you don't think I'm crazy," the woman said, "but my dog is very old and sick. I think maybe I should have her euthanized, but I'm confused about what to do. My family says I'm letting her suffer by keeping her alive, but we've been together nearly eighteen years and

I feel she's not ready to die yet. Can you tell me please, how do you know when it's time to let them go?"

Granted I had heard these words said in slightly different ways many times from people over the past few years. But this woman and her dog, like every individual situation, were unique. They deserved my complete attention and clearest help tailored to their current experience. I offered suggestions based on my own personal experiences, and hoped that I could help Sue come to her own decision, one with which she would feel comfortable.

Sue and I spent the next hour as if old companions, sharing dog stories, and exploring various world philosophies regarding life, death, and beyond. We considered possible choices for her dog, and her own visions, hopes, and dreams. I encouraged her to speak openly with her dog and to just as openly listen for, and accept the answers she would receive. "Your dog will let you know when it's time," I assured Sue.

We discussed the value of letting go, not only the animal in question, but letting go of doubt, fear, guilt, even sorrow. I shared my thoughts on angelic beings and my experience of asking them for help.

Quite naturally and easily we diverged into an exchange of animal jokes and our laughter sparkled amid shared tears. Then spontaneously, we ended our conversation. "Thank you," Sue said, her voice stronger than before. "It's time for me to speak with my dog."

"Yes," I replied. "I have some more listening to do with my own animal crew!"

She promised to let me know the decision regarding her dog. Because she lived nearby, I offered to accompany her to the animal hospital if she decided euthanasia was appropriate. Or, I would come to her home and be supportive should she prefer to have her dog die at home. I would be on call if she needed a shoulder to cry on at any time. And finally, I told her that it was normal for grieving to take some time, but if she left her heart open, another tail-wagging, fur-bearing soul would find her.

In my opinion, euthanasia is one of the most difficult decisions that an animal caregiver must make. I receive many calls from people whose companion has just died and their grief is usually tremendous. However, people calling to ask whether or not they should euthanize an animal companion experience a greater agony just trying to make such a decision.

At such times I can only be a mirror for their own inner truth. Once a veterinarian has been consulted, and perhaps friends or others such as myself, the decision to euthanize an animal must ultimately be a personal one made by the primary caregiver. I cannot say to anyone, "Yes, you need to put your animal friend to sleep, it's time." Conversely, I would never say, "No, it isn't time, you should wait." The choice will be made clearly and concurrently by both the animal and his or her human.

Many lessons on euthanasia have come my way, judging by the number of times I've had to make that final call. With some animals I've struggled through and to this day still hold regrets, while with others I feel totally at peace. Pain and confusion are a part of the process no matter what.

Sometimes there really seems no choice at all, such as when renal failure occurs, which can be extremely painful when accompanied by vomiting. Final and usually painful stages of cancer or other terminal illnesses, and serious injuries due to accidents or abuse are strong calls for euthanasia. But when the choice is not that clear, especially in old animals, I always offer three suggestions that I personally use with great success:

First, I tell the dying creature that it is okay to die. Yes, I will miss her; I will grieve deeply. I would love for her to live forever, but that's not possible. Besides, I know where she's going, it's a great place, and because we've known each other we will never be separated in spirit. *If you need to go,* I say, *go ahead. I support your journey every step of the way.* I also add that I'm going to be just fine in a little while and do not stay around for me.

It is essential to mean every word that is spoken or thought. Animals have shown me time and again that they understand my thoughts more than my spoken words. Animals are highly intelligent, sentient, and clairvoyant, often to a degree far more advanced than humans, though we might not want to admit it. Animals read our intentions and take those for our truth, even if our words belie our heartfelt feelings. If I am saying, "It's okay to let go," but I'm thinking, *Please don't die, I hope you don't die, how can I live without you?* then the animal will, if at all possible, act on the thoughts rather than the words. I have seen animals struggle with great suffering to stay in their bodies until I am ready to let them go. Perhaps animals read the visual images our thoughts and words form, or sense vibrations or colors relative to our emotions. Whatever it is, they pay far more attention to thoughts than spoken words, and almost always will try in their unselfish, compassionate way, to make their death easy for us.

For the **second step** I ask my animal friend for her assistance. Perhaps I might say, "I'm just a bit confused and tired right at the moment. Would you please help me understand as clearly as possible what you want to do?" I will ask the animal, "Are you ready to leave? Would you like some veterinary assistance?"

The **third step** requires that I take some deep breaths to calm and center myself, and without working too hard at it, listen and watch for the response. My experience has shown me that the animal's response always comes, sometimes immediately, but usually some time later when I'm not concentrating so desperately. Sometimes an animal's signal is direct, as was the case when Josie, the goat, was dying. She leaned against the barn wall, her eyes becoming dull. As I witnessed this, a thought was firmly planted in my mind to help her move on. One I couldn't deny. Josie had sent me a strong signal several days before she died, letting me know that release from the severe pain of her cancer was appropriate. However, I was too focused on her physical condition to really listen. Yet, I remember being concerned (as I always am in such cases) that she might be suffering while the doctors and I searched for answers. But Josie waited without complaint, anger, or resentment. She knew, I'm sure, that I was doing the best I could for her at the time. Now I remind myself that our last communication was one of love on my part and gratitude on hers. This memory washes away all the struggle of indecision, and clinging to my fear that I made the wrong decision. What a wonderful way to die, saying, "Thank you."

Arnan, another animal teacher, helped me to understand even further when euthanasia is the merciful answer. She was a domestic White Pekin duck born with severe arthritis. Michael and Tim helped me rescue Arnan and three other ducks from the local county fair when she was just a duckling. Over the years she spent with us, her legs and feet became progressively swollen and malformed. As a result, she learned to hobble along by swinging her large body from side to side. Though difficult for her, and obviously painful during cold, damp weather, Arnan remained cheerful, an endearing characteristic of ducks. Clearly, she enjoyed most aspects of her life and kept a relatively easy pace with the rest of the flock.

About five years later, Arnan's condition suddenly worsened and she was no longer able to move around except by dragging her feet and scraping her body along the frozen ground. This caused her legs and feet to bruise and bleed, and her wing feathers, which she used to balance herself, began to break off.

Enough is enough, I thought. Of course, I never took the time to silence my own thoughts and listen to what *she* wanted. Ever patient and uncomplaining, Arnan dragged herself across the winter ground while I placed repeated calls to a local veterinarian because my regular veterinarian was out of town. I felt it was time to have her euthanized.

Interestingly, the doctor never returned my calls. But while I waited I made Arnan soft, warm nesting places, gave her extra baths in warm water, and plenty to eat and drink beyond her usual daily meals. As days, weeks, and then months passed (was I really still expecting that phone call?) Arnan began to respond to the extra attention and care by once again rising up on those swollen feet and taking a few tentative steps. Intuitively, I felt I should wait and see what would happen next before deciding again to call the vet.

Now basking in mid-summer warmth, Arnan didn't walk far, but seemed satisfied to be hand-carried from her nighttime nest to her daytime place in the soft grass under the maple tree by our back door. There, under my watchful eye she washed herself from a large water bowl, feasted on bugs that wandered by, nibbled fresh leaves and chunks of tomato, and napped contentedly in gentle patches of sunlight. Her flock mates, even some of the chickens, stayed close to her, chatting amiably among themselves and generally letting life drift pleasantly by.

Often throughout those months I thought of how close I had come to having Arnan euthanized. Originally, I had thought euthanasia was merciful in her case, based only on outer physical appearances. I blessed the doctor for never calling back, because if he had, Arnan would not have had the opportunity to continue to enjoy more of life. The situation might have changed at any time and I had come to realize that. Actually, Arnan knew precisely when and what other measures would be called for. On a cool, delightful September day she chose to leave, tucking her soft white head between her wings and simply "stepping out" during sleep, so easily, so gently.

⌒

Marigold, one of my favorite goats, also gave me the gift of learning to listen very carefully. I was told she had a brain tumor. Dr. Dan showed me how pressure from the tumor was pushing her left eye nearly out of the socket. Yet, as the oldest of my ten goats, Marigold was still eating well and full of enough energy to jump fences. Dr. Dan felt she was comfortable, but cautioned me to keep a close watch on her.

A month later I found Marigold lying helplessly on her side in the barn. I eased her up, brushed her off and guided her wobbly body into the hay room where she drank some much-needed water. I assumed one of the other goats had pushed Marigold over as she had always been the "undergoat" of the herd, easily and frequently picked on by the more aggressive members.

Special attention brought Marigold back to normal within a couple of days and I was careful from then on to isolate her as much as possible from the others. But one afternoon while I was trimming hooves, Marigold's granddaughter, Amanda, accidentally ran full speed into Marigold, rupturing her right eye. Now Marigold was nearly blind and in a great deal of pain as well.

Another one of those emotional enough-is-enough moments once again pushed me to the phone. I called Dr. Dan's office and said I was bringing Marigold over to be euthanized. As I was trying to push, lift, shove her 150-pound body into the back of my car, Marigold was munching down on a particularly fine bunch of wild onion grass. Then she moved on to consume an apple Tim had brought to her as a going-away present. Already laden with grief and guilt, and now unsettling misgivings on the whole project at hand, I pulled and pushed one strongly resistant goat into the car. Finally, off we drove, Marigold and I.

Here I was once again, alternately speaking to a goat and to God the entire way over Afton Mountain, a solid thirty-minute trip. I wasn't sure either one was listening. All I wanted was help to get my rampaging thoughts and emotions out of the way in order to understand what was really called for. *Please God, help me understand! Please Marigold, what do you want?*

By the time I pulled into the animal hospital and Dr. Dan came around to the car, Marigold was leaning over the seat, chewing her cud and taking a great deal of interest in the steering wheel. I knew then what I had to do. "I'm taking her home again," I said bravely, flinching just a bit. Surely, Dr. Dan would think I had lost my sanity? Instead, he studied my lop-eared lady, placed a kind hand along her back, and smiled.

"I have to agree with you," he said. "She's not ready to be put to sleep yet. You'll know when it's time." He didn't even charge me for the visit. Back over the mountain we went, me singing and chatting to Marigold as she leaned over the front seat and chewed her cud. We must have been quite a sight.

I'm not sure I ever thanked God for insight and guidance, but I know I thanked my goat. As with all animals I've known and whose judgment I depend on, Marigold was direct, clear, and practical in her answer to my frantic questions. From Monday afternoon when I brought Marigold back home, right up through Friday afternoon it seemed as if she ate more than she had in all her fourteen years: apples, bananas, broccoli, wild onion grass as well as her daily rations of hay, corn, soybean meal, and oats. Marigold's sparse coat began to glow and her stature remained jaunty despite difficulty with vision.

Friday evening at feeding time Marigold was out munching dandelion leaves while I cleaned the barn. I noticed she had begun slowly circling my car, moving in tighter and tighter circles, faster and faster, then randomly bumping into it as she swung around and around. I eased her into her stall, noticed foam trickling from her mouth and the one swollen eye was glassy and partially rolled back.

Marigold was having a seizure caused by the pressure of the tumor on her brain. What I had taken for brutality on the part of the other goats before, really had been a first seizure. I helped Marigold through the spasms and remained with her for most of the evening until I felt sure she was resting comfortably. But by early morning she was again on her side on the floor, bruised and dazed, having suffered through another seizure.

Now I knew without any doubt that enough was enough. This time our drive over the mountain was in the rain and I didn't feel so bright inside myself either. Marigold lay in the back, her eye rolled up, her breathing shallow and irregular. She was already well on her way.

At the office I held Marigold's head in my lap while Dr. Dan administered the merciful injection. I said a quiet prayer, thanked her for the twelve tremendous years she had been in our family, and a magnificent final week. I wished Marigold a joyous journey, fields of celestial honeysuckle, and hugged her one more time. Then her soul was out, sighing with enormous relief, I'm sure, to be free once again.

All the way home I cried, for myself especially. It was my forty-second birthday. How ironic, I thought, it's really Marigold's birthday too, her first into a very special existence.

~

Over the years I have come to appreciate the option of euthanasia, and that there are circumstances where it is a great comfort, though never easy. Each of these situations has brought multiple teachings, each instance helpful in cases that followed, and always offering insight into past experiences that I might not have fully understood at the time. (Later, I share more stories that involve euthanasia.)

The bottom line? Mercy. Learning to ask for guidance, learning to listen to the other, not just myself; helping another despite my own desires and longings, and being truly willing to let go. Mercy requires not doing what is convenient, economical, or practical at the moment, but rather what is called for on a very high level of consideration for another living, sentient being. Mercy might mean administering euthanasia to ease pain and suffering. Or perhaps mercy means offering that extra measure of comfort, support, encouragement, food, or medicine.

To be merciful is to be soft and gentle with myself as well as with the one dying. Mercy is taking the time, making the effort to center myself and find my inner peace. Then I can be still, to listen and accept whatever the animal asks for. Then I am at peace with my decision for euthanasia.

FOUR

The Art of Letting Go

Dawn and dusk sometimes offer colors and light so incredibly beautiful that from habit I want to grab my camera and capture that vision forever. Yet, I have also discovered that when I allow myself to just be present in those lights and colors as they transmute into new tones and hues, I can let go of my desire to "own" them. When I can just let the sky full of colors be, there is an exhilaration that carries me right into the moment. Perhaps it's the feeling skydivers get, or pilots of small aircraft riding the winds, or sailors on the open sea. It's in the letting go, not needing to manipulate or control, but rather to allow the unfolding of events that ultimately offers me the greatest security.

Similarly, when I can let go of cherished beliefs, then I discover so much more. So when someone is dying and I hear and feel myself desperately holding on, whether to my fears, my sorrow, or my pain, I back off just a bit and meditate on the imagery of that changing sky. I recall the peace I feel just letting it be and change as it needs to. Then I refocus that sense of peace into the situation at hand. It's one of the most helpful exercises I can do.

Animals rarely hang on, unless we're begging them to not die. Allowed their own way, they seem to know just when and how to release themselves from their bodies. Oftentimes, despite my own ideas on the subject, they will take matters into their own hands.

Not so long ago, a smallish creature of delicate proportions seemed to just appear from under my station wagon, which was parked in its usual spot in front of the barn. The creature, a young male Mallard duck, had, as further investigation proved, been spotted earlier in the day a half mile down the main road, purposefully trudging on tired feet toward the direction of our farm. I had hoped he had chosen us for our ambiance of love, yet, at the time I suspected his true goal was the various female domesticated ducks in residence here. In hindsight, I have other thoughts.

Little Eddie, as Tim named the duck with ceremony, quickly set his own rules, making it quite clear that as his own master he expected unhindered access to land and sky. Within days Little Eddie had attached himself as chief suitor to Steffie, a petite Khaki Campbell of demur manner.

Steffie and Little Eddie immediately became inseparable, walking side by side, sleeping next to one another with heads tucked back into their wings. They loved paddling round and round together in the kiddie pond under the maple tree. The only times they were apart were when Little Eddie took off for long, high flights across the road, down around the fields, circling lower and lower until he came in for a crash landing next to his beloved. He always seemed to land too far forward on his bill, so I began coaching him. "Head up, Eddie!" I'd shout as he began his descent. Steffie would watch anxiously and I often wondered if she was coaching him as well.

Sometimes he reserved the kiddie pond for his own spectacular display of water sports, making sure, of course, that Steffie was paying attention. And she always seemed suitably impressed. Eddie was the only one of our ducks able, or perhaps willing, to swim underwater, circling the bottom of the pool, then creating enormous waves with his wings. I could always tell which duck was in the water by the degree of splashing.

My family and I kept waiting for Little Eddie to leave — perhaps in the spring when other Mallards returned to the local watering holes; or in the late summer when migration began again. We reminded ourselves that as a wildling, he deserved his freedom.

Eddie was as dramatic in his departure, when it did come, as his arrival a year and a half earlier. Usually a fellow of precise habits, Eddie left Steffie one afternoon on the front lawn at a time of day when he never flew or swam or even foraged for insects. Eddie took off on a long, low flight, down into the road, straight into the side of an oncoming pickup truck.

It was obvious to me, although I could not convince the distraught driver of the truck, that it was time for Eddie to leave on a migration that called him away from physical life. This was no accident. I sensed by the strange break in his routine that Eddie had purpose. I believe he had exercised his options and had followed through on some higher commitment clear only to himself. In a word, Little Eddie knew precisely what he was doing; he always had demonstrated a strong will and intelligence in everything he did.

Steffie, however, was devastated. Not until I laid his body in front of her did she stop looking and calling for him. She walked over to his body, studied it for a moment, then turned away. She ate her dinner and settled down with the rest of the flock. But I worried about Steffie. Ducks mate for life and I knew that when one of a pair died, the other would often follow suit. Losing Eddie was difficult enough for me; I didn't want Stef to go as well, selfish though that was of me, and I told her so.

During the following week Steffie ate well, wandered with the other ducks, swam in the pond. But I sensed something different about her, a loneliness that I hoped I was only imagining in my acute worry for her.

On the Friday morning one week to the day that Eddie left us, I found Steffie in the duck house. She appeared to be resting comfortably with her head tucked back between her wings, eyes closed. She had died sometime in the night.

I felt so sad for my loss of two sweet little ducks. How much I would miss them! But also, I felt exhilarated for their reunion. There was no doubt in my mind that Steffie and Little Eddie were together once again. What a gift to witness such a partnership, a love and loyalty too rarely shared among humans. As a jewel held to the light, Little Eddie dropped in one day and brought me great lessons, then flew "west" to Spirit. Perhaps we will come full circle once again— Little Eddie, Steffie, and I—renewing a bond we all shared.

It was the ambiance of love, the giving and receiving that brought Little Eddie to my sanctuary. In turn, he offered me a powerful lesson in the art of letting go.

When it is my turn to depart, I wouldn't mind knowing with confidence where I'm going. *Choosing* to slip permanently out of my body would be the most comfortable and peaceful way for me to die. If my two little ducks could be so successful at this, and if we have free will, why then is it so difficult for us humans to die in peace?

Maybe we cling to life with too much resistance. Maybe we fight the natural flow of life while having no trust in our own inner wisdom to recognize the most appropriate time for bowing out gracefully. Animals seem to struggle far less against death than humans do. At least this is true for the wild ones. Animals who live closely with humans seem much more sensitive to the intentions, fears, and possessiveness of the people with whom they associate. Perhaps domesticated animals even take on the human attribute of the fear of dying.

When I am working with a dying animal and trying to sort through my own fears, I try to remember what a friend once said, "If you're trying to untangle a mess of knotted string, stop for a moment and study the whole situation. Then, ask the string *and* the knots to work with you. Thank both for doing so, and go to it." That suggestion has served me well, many times. It works. The knots will practically work themselves out and your fingers will know exactly what to do.

Whether dealing with actual or metaphorical knots, the important thing for me to remember is the part about stepping back and considering the string, the knots, and my fingers as intelligent beings who are willing to cooperate with me and the project at hand. If I see all the parts of the project as working together, and bless the work rather than curse it, resistance dissolves and the work is completed in perfect timing, proper order, and to everyone's satisfaction.

Any activity that involves healing, including death and dying work, is best accomplished by following as natural a system as possible, while taking full advantage of the best that traditional and alternative medicine have to offer. That means not resisting the process. It is impossible to fully comprehend anything as enormous as birth, a life-threatening situation, or death. There are so many aspects continually changing, evolving, creating, and recreating on levels that are beyond our means of knowing. In these situations, I have to simply trust that when animals die they intuitively know it's their time to die. Then I can allow them to follow their own sensibilities.

Take that knotted string again. Maybe it's one of my old dogs who's been with me for over sixteen years, dying of congestive heart failure. That's a difficult and painful way to die. So there are lots of knots tying up that string: anxiety on both our parts, my distress to see her in such distress, and her own physical pain in dying. When I step back for a moment and take a few long, deep, steadying breaths, concentrating on the out breath, then I can release tension and relax into the peace of my own inner wisdom. What my years of experience have shown me is that my dog knows what she is doing. I believe she has, in her soul, chosen when and how she will die. I need to trust that, allow that to happen, and tell her so. Then I can say, "It's okay if you want to die right now. I'll support you all the way. Let me know how I can help you." Then I thank my dog for knowing precisely how to handle the situation.

After this initial step, I then have to act on my sense of what needs to be done to help untangle those "knots." I continue to ask my dog what she specifically needs from me and stay attentive to feeling the sensations that often hold the answers. I have made the decision to trust my animal companion, now I must also trust myself.

~

I believe that the one-heart/mind level is the inner wisdom of all beings everywhere. On this level we are keyed into each other, and each of us knows precisely what to do and when. Steffie and Little Eddie seemed to know that, and so did Robyn, a very special friend to me for nearly twelve years. A veteran white hen, her gutsy, jaunty ways had pulled her through several crises, more than any bird should endure. But early one spring a neighbor's dog stopped by and mauled Robyn and another one of our young Rhode Island Red hens, Cory. Cory had been severely tossed around, but appeared to have suffered no physical damage. Yet, as hens tend to do (being extremely sensitive, much like sheep and rabbits) Cory immediately sank into a severe state of shock and depression.

Robyn, however, had sustained some deep bite marks along her back and wings and I was more concerned about her than Cory. Both birds were scooped up and rushed into a quiet room in the house. Robyn, who had long ago become very fond of humans, recognized her name when we called to her softly, and responded with as much enthusiasm as she could, circumstances considered. Cory, on the other hand, being naturally more shy and aloof, resisted any attempts to comfort her.

We tended to any visible wounds on Robyn with the appropriate medicine and then each hen was settled into her own cardboard box lined with soft white cotton cloth. Cotton is a gentle, warming fabric that is light to an animal's body. Many creatures don't care to be surrounded by cloth (hens and ducks definitely do not like to have their feathers touched!) and so I am careful not to add any more stress to the situation while being aware that shock victims need to be kept warm.

Finally, I offered words of encouragement, well wishes, and a short prayer for each hen. We dimmed the lights, put on a continuously playing tape of soft music, and left the hens to rest. Both were hunched down in their boxes as if perching for the night, their beaks resting on the top edge.

I checked on them several times that evening before going to bed. On my last visit I laid a soft cloth over Cory's back as she seemed to shiver slightly. Again, I wished them well and went to bed.

Dawn was clear and serene with a satisfying sense of peace about the house. Immediately on rising I went to check my two girls and found Robyn out of her box, preening her feathers and obviously delighted to see me. Cory, on the other hand, was in the same position I had left her the previous evening, hunched over with the coverlet still draped across her. Her beak rested easily on the edge of the box and her eyes were closed as if she were asleep. She had died.

I have watched many chickens die over the years and most have been wrenching and painful, ending up flat on his or her side, legs stretched out stiffly and eyes wide open. Not so with Cory. From her peaceful appearance, I knew she had simply let go of her body and headed off to new adventures in another realm.

In a true sense, both hens survived, each healing in her own way according to natural choices. Without resistance to living, Robyn apparently chose to stay around and had the strength to do so, despite her physical wounds. In fact, she lived another five years, eventually choosing a slow and peaceful withdrawal from life when she was eleven. Cory, without resistance to dying, chose departure without struggle. I had to trust that each hen knew what was right for her and knew where she wanted to be. And maybe they are both still with us, scratching for ethereal bugs, clipping off invisible leaf ends, and having the time of their lives.

FIVE

Releasing Waggy

O f all the creatures who have come to teach me about death and dying, none has led me so deep into the process as did a floppy-eared, black-and-tan dog named Waggy. She forced me to face agonizing choices and learn to take responsibility for my thoughts and actions. Her lesson plan was brutally difficult; I nearly flunked several times, and her determination to help me expand my awareness was fierce. All the while Waggy was never without mercy, tenderness, and love for me. During her last year, through our shared pain and joy, and my final awakening, we grew so close that it felt as if our souls dissolved into the knowing of our common ground. While I was the stubborn student, Waggy was the master, much more than any other being, human or animal, who has entered my journey through this life.

When considering the metaphor of a knotted string, who would disagree that cancer presents one of the most frightening, frustrating, and complicated of all situations? The word cancer is synonymous in most human minds with hopelessness, despair, victimization, and death. Waggy developed cancer when she was twelve years old. She had enjoyed an exceptionally healthy life except for two critical accidents, one involving rat poison in a local apple orchard, and another with a stick in a river. She seemed to walk through these two life-threatening situations with no long-term damage. Her coat was always shiny, she never had fleas, no ear infections, or stomach upsets. Why, then, suddenly cancer?

The cancer was along her gum line on the right side of her mouth and the surgery was difficult. Dr. Partridge felt confident that he had removed all of the tumor, but there were no guarantees, of course. I brought Waggy home from the hospital on the weekend and together we began the process of convalescence; small, almost liquid meals, antibiotics, extra vitamins, warm blankets, and large doses of love and encouragement.

I remember the anger and shock I felt when the rest of my family came home that first night after Waggy's return, with pizza and videos and sat around the television as if all was normal. Too worried about Waggy to consider even eating, and too overwhelmed with the severity of her condition, I couldn't understand how anyone who had lived with this dog for twelve years as they had, could take it all with no concern. Didn't they realize she had cancer?

Of course, Waggy never complained or judged or fretted about the family's reaction. Nor did she demand my attention or anybody else's. She lay on her bed and let me care for her, licking my hand or face in response. When one of my human family would take a break from the current movie and come in to see her, she would reach up and lick his hand as well. I thought I had a lot to fight against, and to be angry and sad about. I was well aware of the odds the cancer would return. Resentment was mine and I felt fully justified. Waggy could have had all those excuses too, plus she bore the pain of surgery. So why wasn't she angry or even depressed?

She recovered quickly from the surgery and in a few days was back out on her walks with me in the woods, sniffing out squirrels and digging up bones. She automatically shifted all her chewing to her left side and returned to enjoying her meals of special kibble, chopped baked chicken, scrambled eggs, biscuits and other such treats. Together we welcomed spring peepers, daffodils and tulips, new leaves on the trees, and the return of robins and hummingbirds.

Late June, during one of my weekly inspections of her mouth, I discovered new tumors. They were tiny, raw, and frightening in their sudden explosion along her gum line, even on the left side now. Dr. Partridge was distressed and very kind. "Yes," he said, "cancer, if it returns, tends to do so with a vengeance; there's really nothing more I can do for her." We discussed Waggy's options, the prognosis, and quality of life. None of it was encouraging. Waggy would not recover, but would probably be comfortable and out of pain until September. But the worst part of the news was that I would have to make the decision when to end her suffering. The chances were that the pain would become too severe long before the cancer itself would take her life.

As I drove home with Waggy I cried all the way, overwhelmed by feelings of failure and victimization. On our next walk in the woods, while she flushed out squirrels, I resolved to heal her. There were cases of spontaneous remission, I told myself, even miracles, so why not for Waggy? I was determined that this dog was not going to die! Over the following months, as the cancer grew larger and more ugly, I studied and tried everything, including energy work, prayer, herbs, and vitamins. Our good friends, Bud and Beverly, introduced me to Essiac, an herbal mixture that has been known to completely cure certain cancers, and although Waggy didn't particularly care for the taste, she lapped several teaspoons of the mixture three times a day. It was almost as if she were simply pleasing me.

People sent Waggy get-well cards, and I read them all to her. Friends called to see how she was doing, I gave her their messages. I hugged Waggy a lot, played music and chanting tapes known for their healing qualities, sang to her, and spoke of being well and sending the cancer away. Waggy always listened intently. For her I pulled out all the stops; I was going to beat this monster devouring my friend. I tried hating the cancer away, then when that didn't feel appropriate, I tried surrounding it with love, visualizing white light dissolving it.

But nothing worked. The cancer continued to grow and spread and by early September was now protruding out the right side of her mouth. It was the most vile thing I had ever seen. The necrotic flesh smelled and she had to be in pain. But not once did Waggy show it. How could I possibly terminate her life when she still enjoyed her walks, chased squirrels, bathed the cats, ate her meals with delight and ease, and was up and ready to welcome all people who came through the door? Even at twelve, a respectable age for a dog her size (still a hefty sixty pounds), she was energetic, alert, and good-natured.

I continued to be self-pitying and angry. Why wouldn't the cancer respond to any treatments? I was racing against an enemy and the enemy was winning. But I had one last option and I staked all my hopes and, sadly, beliefs in it working.

Shortly before Waggy was first diagnosed, I learned of a woman in New England who claimed to be an animal communicator. According to her, she could not only understand the animals and they understand her, but she was able to intuit what they might need homeopathically and otherwise heal the animals of whatever ailed them. I was familiar with other animal communicators who came highly recommended and whom I respected.

Interspecies communication is a rapidly growing field that offers enormous assistance to both humans and nonhumans. Insight provided by such communication clearly demonstrates the intelligence and wisdom of animals and opens new opportunities for all species to be supportive and respectful of one another. I consider consultations with a reputable animal communicator to be an invaluable tool. However, when I first heard about this particular communicator, I was unsure of her credentials, and besides, Dr. Partridge was optimistic about the surgery. So I put the animal communicator out of my mind and concentrated on more traditional forms of treatment.

By the time the cancer returned I had completely forgotten about the New England communicator until that September when I felt I had run out of healing options. I called her and we talked at length.

Every indication she gave me from her "speaking" with Waggy was that my dog wasn't ready to die, didn't want to die, and could easily be cured with certain homeopathic remedies. I ordered them immediately from a company she recommended and waited impatiently for their arrival. Time was running away, I was frantic.

Shortly after that, when I heard that this person had decided to come to Virginia to hold a workshop and do a series of private consultations relative to animal communication, my expectations rose to a high-pitch. This woman promised to come and personally heal my dog!

But from the moment I first heard her speak, I began to sense she might be a fraud. There was that familiar uneasiness in my stomach that I have learned from previous experiences to be a warning signal. Yet, my overwhelming desire to have Waggy healed left me blind and deaf to my intuition.

Because I had invested all my desires for Waggy's recovery in this one unknown person, one of the most agonizing times of my life began. With each of the next three meetings with the animal communicator, two of them with her "working on" Waggy, as she called it, my cherished sense of hope quickly unraveled into despair. I could no longer deny that this woman was incapable of healing my beloved Waggy.

The most compelling evidence against this purported healer was the way my husky-shepherd, Sam, responded to her. Sam was very clear that he did not want the animal communicator on the property. In Sam's thirteen years with us, he has made himself my personal protector and I learned to trust his judgment regarding visitors. He had been brutally and repeatedly beaten and kicked by men before coming to live with us. As a result, he is slow to befriend any visiting and unfamiliar men. Sam seems less concerned with women, however, so his obvious disapproval of the animal communicator was worth noting. The feeling was mutual. She did not like Sam, and demanded that he be removed to a separate room. Sam became fierce and frantic, barking and growling. The afternoon became very unpleasant and confusing for me. Why would an animal as wise and loving as Sam, instantly be on guard against a person claiming to be such an outstanding healer and animal communicator? I found myself listening to Sam despite my desire to have Waggy healed.

During the animal communicator's stay in Virginia, many other people who, like myself, relied on her presumed expertise, suffered. She charged enormous amounts of money for false communication and healing work, enraging most who sought her help. Yet in my mind, it was I who had failed again. My depression and hopelessness flared.

The New England communicator seems to be an unusual case. Since Waggy's death I have often called upon the services of several fine animal communicators who have, without exception, proven their ability and validity in the remarkable field of interspecies communication. Their compassion puts the needs of the animals and their human care-givers before monetary gain. (Some animal communicators I trust and recommend are listed in Resources on page 159.)

Somewhere during that incredible month of October, Waggy spoke to me, not in words or other sounds, but in thought. Perhaps I was finally "hearing" what she had been telling me all along. She told me to let go. Waggy clearly communicated that she would not recover physically.

Intuitively, I knew Waggy was demonstrating through her life, and impending death, that there was perfection and purpose to all that was happening. Each life is part of that mysterious Plan that involves evolution through learning and teaching, growth, expansion, and enlightenment. Yes, dogs included, and certainly humans! Cancer was Waggy's way of fulfilling that learning/teaching that so intricately involved me. Death itself was not the issue; Waggy had fully accepted this. Now it was my turn.

After that realization, I gave up my fight and changed my focus, although for awhile I still held too tightly to fear, despair, and that sense of personal failure. Metaphysicians tell us, "Be in the world but not of it." Sometimes though, the world has to grip me tightly and mercilessly until I am choked into submission. Finally, exhausted and empty except for the great love I felt for Waggy, I once again spoke to her, gave her my blessing to leave when she was ready, and released her from my battle. This time I let go, not in defeat, but to join her in acceptance. I opened my heart to whatever would be called for next.

The next challenging lesson was knowing *when* to let Waggy go. For the rest of October and most of November I agonized over whether it was time to end her pain. Still, she ate well, but more slowly; enjoyed her walks, but let some squirrels go on by. She rested more and it was harder to wake from her naps. Waggy no longer made those great happy sweeps with her tail that earned her name. I knew she was preparing to die; I let her lead. It was the best I could do for her now and I told her so. Many times I asked Waggy to let me clearly know when she had had enough. While I grieved, Waggy remained cheerful, attentive, and appreciative of the love so many people gave her.

The moment I woke on the Tuesday before Thanksgiving I knew it was time to let Waggy go. All the indecision of the past months seemed to have miraculously evaporated and only peace remained. I went downstairs to where Waggy was still sleeping in her favorite chair and she raised her head. "I know," I whispered, "it's time." Later in the morning she went as usual with me to the barn, but instead of exploring as she had just the day before, she lay down in the hay and simply watched me. When I went to hang out the laundry, I turned and saw her moving slowly towards me, her head slightly down and her tail swinging wide and high. "Oh Waggy," I cried, kneeling down to her, "you're telling me it's all right, aren't you!" And her tail moved faster.

Another journey over Afton Mountain with a dying animal, but this trip was remarkable. Usually, Waggy would sit in the passenger's seat, looking intently out the window. This time she chose to sit right next to me, her head resting on the back of the seat by my shoulder. I knew she understood what was happening, so I told her how brave she was, how much I had learned from her, how much I would miss her. I wished her a joyous adventure into the afterlife and beyond, and promised to look her up when I got there myself, or watch for her here if she decided to return.

At the door to the animal hospital, Waggy suddenly began to balk, digging in her feet and shaking badly. Gently I told her, "If I can do this, so can you; we're in it together." I picked her up, all sixty pounds, and carried her into the building and to the examining table. While we waited for Dr. Partridge, I sensed fear rising in Waggy. She had begun to tremble again and her eyes were wide and frantic. I hugged her close to me, asked her to remember all she had taught me over the past year about letting go, and allowing the whole process of life to unfold. "It's so beautiful where you're going," I reminded her, "and there won't be any more pain or weariness."

Silently I began massaging her shoulders and back in large circles, breathing into the circles, matching my breath to hers and then carefully slowing mine as I gently lifted and moved her skin under my fingers. As I focused all my attention on the touch, clearing my mind of past or future oriented thoughts, Waggy immediately began to breathe more easily and slowly, her muscles relaxed, and her eyes became clear and calm again. In Waggy's last moments following the injection, she laid her head back in my arms and peacefully let go of her body.

Since then I have thought often of the many lessons Waggy so patiently taught me. I learned more about my anger and fear and how they can be destructive. I also learned more about when treatment is appropriate, and when release is called for. Through Waggy I learned that relying on someone else so totally, especially of questionable credentials, without trusting my own intuition, never works. Waggy showed me that the disease or condition is not "bad" and we don't have to consider ourselves victims either when afflicted, or when caring for someone who is afflicted.

So often illness is an essential means of expansion into the knowledge of one's true self. When one works with an illness emotionally, mentally, and spiritually, this becomes as critical to healing as any physical work. Waggy demonstrated that healing is not the same as curing; that there is wisdom in knowing when it is time to die and to do so with honor and grace. She also assured me that no matter how courageous one is, sometimes fear, powerful as it is, can override that courage and that is not "bad" either. Fear is part of being in material form on Earth. This confirmed for me the importance of being with someone, animal or human, as they move through dying, and supporting them through the process. In essence, it was Waggy who convinced me to begin serious study of what happens just prior to and during death, and what lies beyond.

Above all, Waggy offered me so many opportunities to practice compassion toward her, which was easy. She also taught me to have compassion for myself, which was difficult, and toward the fraudulent animal communicator, which was close to impossible. I'm still working on that one! Yet I have always known the wisdom of accomplishing new levels of compassion and vow to continue to do so.

In one turbulent year Waggy left me with many gifts, moments, insights, treasures of love, and understanding that are unequalled in all the rest of my experiences. True to form, Waggy gave me one more gift thirteen months after her death. This one was the most spectacular of all.

A December morning just before dawn, no one else was awake in the house except the cats waiting in the kitchen for breakfast. As I moved from the kitchen, through the darkened living room towards the stairs, I saw Waggy. She was sitting straight and radiant just behind the wooden rocker. How beautiful she was! Her black coat glistened, her ears flopped half over as they had in life. She was the image of perfect health and joy, and she was watching me intently. A momentary vision, she was there and gone, leaving a strong message: *Yes, I am — always now — fine. See Rita, I told you there was life after death, and no, I have not and never will leave you in my love for you. Keep up the good work, I'll see you again.*

Had this appearance come right after her death I would have assumed it was my sad and active imagination trying to construct inner peace from it all. However, being so long after Waggy's death, I have absolutely no doubt that her return, brief though it was, was valid. How much I would love to see her again, and to see every one of the animals who has graced my life and then moved on. But for now I will be satisfied that Waggy has spoken for all the people and animals everywhere.

To honor Waggy's efforts, I relate this after-death story to everyone who calls for help with a dying animal. Usually I am still self-conscious enough that I begin by saying, "You're probably going to think I'm crazy, but …." Every person has been grateful for the sharing, and everyone has come away comforted.

I have had many animal teachers since Waggy, each learning process building on the previous ones, each guiding me forward into the next. But Waggy's masterful guidance stands apart because the healing for which I had hoped for so desperately came after all: ultimately to Waggy, and to my own life's work.

SIX

Sadie's Bridge

If I had ever doubted that there is more to an animal than the physical body, Waggy's appearance in my living room more than a year after her death changed my mind. I had always intellectually believed that there is spirit or soul that moves forward once the body dies, but I needed the proof Waggy's spirit gave me to be assured.

From the time of Waggy's appearance, my questions changed. I no longer wonder *if* my animal friends live on after death. Instead, I wonder, *What is that portion of life that rises as the form falls away, and where does "it" go? How can I help the soul leave with as little trauma as possible? How do I then put my own life back together? Can we, who must remain behind, see the soul?*

Some people say they have seen the soul. So, why can't I, especially if I hold so much love for the animal who has just died? Over time, answers flow piece by piece through the animals who offer themselves as my teachers.

Even before Waggy's "return," I noticed at nearly every animal's passing a distinct cessation of life on the physical plane while sensing new movement on a far more expansive level. But there have been instances when an animal has died and I felt nothing. The first time this happened, I fell rapidly into a dark depression for the first time in my life, doubting everything I had always believed. Could I have been mistaken about life existing after death? And, of course, the harder I looked for signs of a continuing soul, the less I saw or heard or felt.

It took six months to shed the doubt and thus the pain, and begin my slow climb towards understanding again. I had to admit that while I may think I am advancing in knowledge with each experience, truthfully, such setbacks cause me to shift and refine many of my beliefs. Repeatedly, I am humbled by the mystery of life and death and the beyond. When doubt resurfaces from time to time, and I am able to relax into the doubt rather than fight it, new understanding begins to appear.

For instance, in the case of the dying baby birds I describe in Chapter Two, a most unusual experience unfolded at the same time. One of my favorite wildflowers is wild mustard, the plant I unexpectedly saw that day as I carried the baby bird behind the barn. A wild mustard plant would not have gone unnoticed, especially since I walk through that field twice a day putting the donkeys in and out of their pasture. Without any doubt, I knew that plant had not been there thirty minutes before. Had it been called into being by some force or energy beyond my comprehension? Was its immediate purpose in time/space to serve the ultimate healing of a small suffering bird? Obviously, I was also enmeshed in that purpose. Had the same force called my attention to the birds, guided my heart and intuition, led me around the barn? Was the compassion I felt for the bird a powerful motivator that energized all the other elements in the unfolding process of the creature's release from her body?

Later that day, I began reading *Rolling Thunder*, a book by Doug Boyd about a Shoshone Medicine Man whom I had been wanting to learn about for some time. When I reached page nine I read, "Often herbs just appear where they are needed...." In retrospect, everything that happened that day flowed in an easy, synchronized rhythm, without formal ritual, begging, or resistance on my part. Once again I realized that death can bring for both the care giver and the one dying, healing.

Sometimes the understanding can come from an encounter with a friend who has just lost a parent and has experienced a visitation from him or her afterwards. Perhaps a piece of artwork, a poem, or a greeting card can reflect the image and/or personality of the animal who has just died. Many times I ask myself, *Are these coincidences? Or am I being sent messages or signs, telling me, as did Waggy, that life continues in another dimension?*

I believe that the energy form I call "soul" moves through a process not unlike the experience of birth into the physical world. Death is the soul's journey across a mysterious bridge that connects the physical and the ethereal. Those who have had a near-death experience appreciate such a passage and describe it as luminous, edgeless, timeless, fluid, and filled with such sound, tone, color, and light as never fully experienced by those of us currently still in our bodies. Usually, such people return from a near-death experience no longer afraid of death and what lies beyond. The rest of us can only wonder, trust, and catch glimpses of such magnificence. Dying and death are a journey that do not deserve all the fear and despair we give it.

⌣

Sadie's death took me into a more complex understanding of the process of crossing that bridge. Fortunately, by the time Sadie was ready to move on I had a clearer understanding about the release of the soul. Yet I had built such a strong relationship with this particular companion, letting go was harder than ever before.

Sadie had joined our household two weeks before Michael's birth. I'm not sure what I was thinking when I adopted a six-week-old puppy just before the birth of my first child. Impetuousness has always been my driving force, so often my redeemer as well. And Sadie certainly proved to be our redeeming factor many times in all those years! Nanny to our two boys, she guided us with ease and wisdom through crisis after crisis. Sadie was there in quiet support through two years of unemployment. She stood by us when a construction accident left Doug blind in one eye, forcing our move from New England. She mothered all those homeless creatures of various species who found us, and she graciously shared our love and attention for so many in need. Sadie exemplified unconditional love for all her family.

Because of her advanced age, I knew that Sadie would never be well again. Yet, I couldn't say goodbye. The vibration of the word alone sent thunderclaps throughout my body. My beloved Sadie, companion for more than seventeen years, was ready to be free from her frail frame and exhausted heart. I felt confident about where she was headed, yet I did not want to let her go!

How does one let go of such a companion? All philosophical conjecturing about life and death aside, in the end I would be left with a lifeless body. Sadie would be obscured to my physical senses of sight, sound, and touch. Oh, I knew I would mend and I was certain many would follow her trail to our sanctuary. Yet at the moment of Sadie's dying, all that meant nothing.

However, it was Sadie's passing that opened the door to a new under-standing of the concept of energy beyond our physical world. Barbara Ann Brennan, a pioneer in healing with energy fields, talks about the Universal Energy Field (UEF) in her book, *Hands of Light*, and in her recent book, *Light Emerging*. Known in ancient cultures, the UEF has been called *Prana* (in India) and *Chi* (in China). This energy, according to Brennan, "Permeates all space, animate and inanimate objects, and connects all objects to each other." Furthermore, she writes, "Investigators of this field state that the UEF is basically synergistic, meaning the simultaneous action of separate agencies that together have greater total effect than the sum of their individual effects." This belief in a universal energy field allows me to join the energy of the animals and people I have known who have died, and form an eternal bond. Sometimes I am even able to communicate with them through this bond. I know beyond any doubt that they do indeed continue to exist, even though the body has died.

I wonder if the UEF is the Oneness we hear so much about. Perhaps this is where souls such as Sadie and myself, companions in physical life, blend and become more than we are individually. Brennan notes, "The UEF exists in more than three dimensions...It is synergistic and builds form...It seems that it is always continuing to build form."

Gary Zukav also acknowledges this universal energy in his book, *The Seat of the Soul.* "The Light that flows through your system," he says, "is Universal Energy. It is the Light of the Universe. You give that Light form."

Increasingly, I am able to access the UEF through centering, mindfulness meditation practice (also called Insight Meditation, or *Vipassana* in the Buddhist tradition), and being open to all possibilities. Many years ago I discovered that simply by being still and focusing my attention inward, I could tap into wisdom that always provided the direction, the comfort, the courage, and the strength I needed. Such "communication" comes to me as thought, just as if I were having an ordinary conversation, but instead of an external dialogue, it is as if I am conversing with my own higher self or perhaps my guardian angel. This compassionate wisdom broadens my approaches and views to every thing in life.

⌒

Death is not the final word. Nor need it be frightening. As with everything else in life, one's attitude toward death and what follows determines any direct or indirect experience with it. Death is simply the movement of energy from one form of existence into another, much like water becoming ice, steam, or vapor.

My life experiences teach me that this is true for all beings. Energy passes through various stages, forms, or bodies. There is a physical, material body and a subtle, or energy body that surrounds and permeates every being. This body, (also known as the aura, or energy field), has been documented by Kirlian photography where auras are seen around living beings as well as around inanimate objects. Both energy "bodies," material and subtle, are in a continual process of transformation, since physicists tell us that energy can neither be created nor destroyed.

As I see it, the love and respect Sadie and I shared for one another produced an energy of even greater magnitude than we each possessed alone. This love was so expansive that by virtue of the universal energy field, it positively affected the interconnected energy of all of life everywhere. Such a concept certainly has made me more conscious of my thoughts, words and actions, realizing the impact each has on the whole of creation.

When I bond with Sadie, or Waggy, or anyone else, that expansive energy we form can never be destroyed. Was the energy that brought Waggy's soul back in that instant a reminder that one is never truly "dead" as we understand the term, but instead remains very much alive, only in an alternative energy form?

But what is this new form? Certainly it is not as I knew them in their physical bodies despite how solid Waggy may have looked behind that chair. Rather I believe it to be an exquisite combination of the love and respect we shared in what scientists call "sympathetic resonance." And by virtue of that sharing, this new soul-energy-form becomes integrated into, and inseparable from, my soul and that of my animal companion, creating a more highly evolved soul within each — a reflection of each other. Death, then, cannot possibly be considered "the end." Nor can anyone who has died be considered "lost."

Though I was still so new to this way of thinking, I knew Sadie would evolve into a new form. I had just begun communications with my inner "angel" and stumbled more than walked through the process. Yet, when Sadie lay there, her last breath barely felt by my hand, I sensed the need to turn inward and in the ensuing silence, heard these thoughts:

She will greet you on the other side, but first you have to let her go. Acknowledge her passing. She will not die until you do so, and soon she will be in very great pain.

I hesitated, still so attached to Sadie's physical presence. "But I love her," I fussed. "I can't bear to say goodbye."

Of course, came the answer. *That is absolutely normal and I wouldn't want you to feel any other way. Still, the physical body has to separate from her soul if either she or you are to progress in your journeys. She's asking for permission to go, but then, she's not really going anywhere, not just yet. She will wait for you for awhile on this (etheric) side.*

"Yes," I said, but not so sure of myself. Yet, how could I hold her back? Had she ever held me back all our years together? I could at least give her my blessing for release. And so I did, through those blasted, inevitable tears. "Go, Sadie, it's okay. I love you. I'll be fine."

Immediately I felt her heart beat slower, the breath soften and stop, the body sink into peace. And Sadie was gone.

"Now what do you say?" I heard most distinctly in my soggy brain, uncertain of the message.

Feeling a bit cranky and exhausted, I mumbled something impolite. Inner guidance aside, I, the human, ached.

But the response was gentle: "Hello. Say, hello!"

I looked up from Sadie's body in disbelief. I had carried her body out under her favorite tree near the garden where I would eventually bury her. I didn't see Sadie's soul, but the air sparkled and I knew beyond doubt that she and my beloved angel were right beside me.

"Hello, Sadie!" I said happily.

As with my encounter with Waggy after her death, Sadie didn't stay long. Soon the sparkling, dancing energy that was her soul, dissipated, leaving a warmth and joy that permeated my entire being. I knew Sadie was free; I knew she was well; and I knew she lived endlessly. Without a shred of doubt, I knew in that brief meeting beyond the physical boundaries, Sadie and I had become one energy of far greater proportion, or power, than we had ever been before.

That infallible source of wisdom that I discovered with Sadie's passing is always here. I don't turn to it as much these days as I want to. I get busy and forget, until a gentle nudge reawakens me to that perfect presence.

SEVEN

Common Ground

Every late October in Virginia, the ladybugs come by the hundreds to seek shelter from the encroaching winter. Clouds of the tiny creatures gather at the windows, come in on the dogs and cats, attach to my clothing, or crawl through the smallest of cracks to eventually hibernate in clusters on the ceilings until spring. While many people I know object to them, I enjoy their company and they have yet to prove offensive. I have heard accounts of them biting, letting off terrible odors, and chewing upholstery, but none of these things have happened at my house.

My only objection to their arrival is the tedious task of stepping around them as they jog across the floor, or fishing them out of soapy dishwater when they insist on falling in, or rescuing them from being crushed beneath the paws of interested cats. Fragile creatures, ladybugs have no sense of danger nor do they seem to care whether an obstacle such as a wall, is in their path. They simply climb up, over, and keep going.

Hopefully, their attitude toward life-ending experiences is as nonchalant and cheerful, because with the numbers that abound here, ladybug mortality runs rather high. No one is randomly, absent-mindedly or intentionally destroyed. It just happens. And I take each passing seriously. The ladybugs die without apparent concern, tucking their tiny feet within their shells and without regret, simply depart. At least it would seem so. On the other hand, I must stop and bless each passing, wishing happy journeys and clear light. And as I move the small being to a potted plant for a final resting place I sense an energy flowing from me, with them, as they travel forth. Most people would think this is a lot of effort for a so-called "insignificant" insect. But for me, it is simply the conscious activation of our common ground of love and compassion.

But before I could even begin to understand or relate to the common ground that I share with all life, I had to begin with myself. I had to come to at least a minimal understanding of who I am, especially with animals in need. Trying to work from a foundation of fear, confusion, and grief caused nothing but more turmoil and a sense of isolation from the one I was trying to help. Intuitively I felt that if I could go within and beyond my own turmoil, I would find another foundation, another place of peace and balance.

My initial efforts to find that place were often desperately painful. Initially, they drew me all the way back to the age of five when I was confronted with my first lesson regarding issues of life and death. Then, my teacher was a small tree. My mother, sister, and I had recently traveled to Connecticut from Texas to live with my grandmother after my parents' divorce. Although I found great adventure in the move, I also felt a grave uneasiness. At five, I was not yet capable of understanding just where my father had gone, or why. When our mother sat us down on my older sister's new bed and said, "Your father won't be living with us anymore," Sylvie cried. However, I continued to play with my stuffed animals, apparently burying the loneliness and sense of his desertion deep inside me.

Because there were no other children my age in the neighborhood, animals, flowers, and trees as well as imaginary beings, became my closest friends. A young hemlock by the front gate was my favorite companion. The tree offered shelter during rain or snow and became my Lookout Man for endless games of Indians (I didn't care much for cowboys). My tree friend was most gracious and eager to please.

Our first summer in Connecticut, for reasons I couldn't fathom at such a young age, my grandmother felt it best to remove my companion, the hemlock. Despite my begging and tantrums, Walter, the handyman, quite unceremoniously chopped down the little tree and carried "him" off to the brush pile at the back of the house. It was a brutal end to a friendship, a ragged end without heart from either Walter or my grandmother, even though I wrapped my small arms around the trunk where he lay and sobbed my goodbyes. In fact, I openly mourned the loss of that little tree more than that of my father.

Of course, on some level I knew my father had "died" as well, had ruthlessly whacked himself from my life without ceremony or explanation on his part. But it was I who had been thrown on the brush pile. So, even at five years old I was trying to figure out the whole mess of someone important to me being here one moment and gone into oblivion the next. I was furious with the senselessness of the act and the blatant disregard for a living thing. To my mind the whole situation, father and tree, was outrageous and unacceptable. To this day I never have let go of my indignation nor my fierce loyalty to tree and truth.

Much later I was able to better understand my grandmother's reason for cutting down my friend and companion. It seemed that the local town drunks had taken to bedding down in the thick hedges that separated our house from the street. My grandmother feared that one of them might lurk behind the hemlock and with no good intentions, leap out at any one of us as we passed through the gate.

I can accept this now and bless my grandmother who also was one of my best friends all my growing years. And I thank my beloved tree for expanding my horizons regarding life versus death, and practicality and fear versus wisdom and compassion. But over the years there have been questions I have thought about: *Was there another solution to the problem of the vagrants? Could my little friend have been spared such a blunt and premature death? Was it necessary to throw him so disrespectfully on the brush pile with no concern for the pain and confusion he must have felt? And my pain and confusion, obvious to all the humans in my family, why wasn't it addressed? What of ceremony, gratitude, processing of grief? And what was it that the tree and I shared that meant so much to me?*

Such questions have helped form the foundation for my own life philosophy and ethics. Ultimately, these questions have lead me to discover and better understand the concept of a common ground — that place of peace that all beings share.

As I continued my search throughout the years for my so-called original, or true, nature, I was led back through dreams and meditation, even before my present birth. I learned that I was far more than my present physical form and personality. I sensed that I was not just a soul experiencing a current physical life. I have come to believe that each aspect of myself — past, present, and future "selves," — must have purpose and meaning, interblending to form who I am at any moment, at any place.

From early connections to the animal kingdom and to my tree companion, I had no doubt that all beings experience and share the same incredible interaction of body and soul. When I am able to find that place of inner peace within myself, I can be in communion with that same sacred place within all others, including animals. Yet, even with such knowledge, when a beloved animal companion is in pain and dying, I often find it very difficult to see beyond the animal's physical appearance to his or her wholeness. But through experience I have learned that if I focus on the love and compassion I feel for the animal, rather than fear, sorrow, or frustration, then I find our common ground, the sacred common denominator of all beings.

Often, when I am helping the dying, that is when the most profound experience of sharing common ground occurs. For example, when my old dog Waggy died, I was present for her during her transition. Our apparent separate existences in different bodies became absorbed in the process of her dying and in the process of my helping. Loving kindness and compassion brought us into union. The caregiver and the one in need each become giver/receiver of that profound gift called love. And in the giving and the receiving of love we both have the opportunity to heal. In particular, there have been two beings who have greatly magnified my understanding of our common ground: Corky, a dog, and Jeffrey, a child.

Corky was born under our house and graced my life for over fifteen years. One day past her fifteenth birthday, Corky eased into her death. My friend Harriet telephoned from North Carolina to thank me for the photograph taken of Corky just days before her passing. "She looks so intelligent," Harriet remarked. We then discussed what had been Corky's physical and mental condition since birth, of which Harriet had not previously been aware, and we agreed, the photograph showed the true Corky, fully emerged.

My relationship with Corky was special from the beginning, in particular because from birth she was severely mentally challenged, although the currently accepted terminology would say she was "exceptional." I have to say that both terms applied. There were many habits, instinctive and easy for a so-called normal dog, that challenged Corky greatly: climbing or descending stairs; going in and out of doorways without crashing headlong into the door frame; drinking water without first submerging the nose and inhaling; barking, knowing something was there, but not quite getting the accurate direction in which to bark. Frequently, I would find Corky sitting in the water dish or her food bowl, looking frantically for her food or water and not having the slightest clue that it was under her. Once, when she was hospitalized, Dr. Partridge asked me incredulously if I knew she threw her food dish around. Oh yes, I replied. At that time she was on her third bowl, each successive one completely chewed through around the rim. And they were stainless steel!

Anyone who knew Corky will testify that through her intense physical experience rose *wisdom*. This kind of wisdom cannot accurately be conveyed through the spoken or written word. But when privileged to know and perhaps care for someone like Corky, one knows without needing to prove or have proof, that one has stood fully in the presence of Spirit.

Many years before Corky was born, I took care of a little boy, Jeffrey, while his mother worked outside the home. At eight years old, this child had advanced degenerative disease and had outlived his medically predicted life span by two years. When we met, Jeffrey was completely blind, nearly deaf, and was unable to do anything except feed himself, and that with difficulty. The first time his mother led Jeffrey up the sidewalk to our door, I was terrified of him. To me, he seemed enormous for his age, his head and hands, clubby, and distorted. He rocked back and forth bellowing, the only recognizable word being "Bye-bye," which he repeated frequently.

Within our first week together, I became aware of the intense energy of love flowing unrestrained and fearlessly from Jeffrey, and in the year that I cared for him, we became devoted to one another. As I held this youngster on my lap, we would laugh together for the joy he found in everything. He learned to say without my prompting, "I love you," and then so quietly, "Bye-bye." Jeffrey taught me through the wisdom of courage, laughter, joy and supreme peace. Though long since gone from this life, two decades later Jeffrey still is one of my finest teachers about life and living. He remains, in my memory, as one of the dearest human friends I have ever known.

The experience of Jeffrey came, blossomed, moved on, and as with all life, mellowed into memory, becoming an integral part of who I am. And so later did my experience with Corky, the same kind of little being as Jeffrey, so often confused, distracted, lost in a world whirling endlessly around her. Half in apology, although constantly aware of her special qualities, I would always explain to those meeting Corky for the first time that she was mentally challenged. But it was Barb, veterinary technician at the animal hospital, who helped me change the habit and I am grateful to her for that. "You know," she said, standing back a bit and looking so kindly and thoughtfully at Corky on the examining table, "I really believe those whom we think of as mentally retarded are possibly the 'normal' ones; we are the ones who have lost touch with *true* reality."

How perfectly she voiced all that I had experienced with Jeffrey and was re-experiencing with Corky. Indeed, both child and dog had given me a brief but stunning glimpse of a magnificent realm of being that knows no comparison in our so-called sane world.

It took my friend Harriet's observation of Corky's intelligence to focus that which I had always sensed: that beyond the illusion of the physical form, no matter how we try to label it, shines our true nature, which is truly indefinable, uncontainable, undiminishable by circumstance, or mental and physical condition. Our true nature cannot be touched by the process of aging or by abuse, neglect or the ignorance of another.

Perhaps the Jeffreys and Corkys of the world are here to remind us through their own unhindered expression of their soul, that despite appearances or dramatic changes, there always remains the steady "hand" of that common ground. For me, this is a comforting thought especially in those desperate times.

A child and a dog, "not quite right" as the saying sadly and inaccurately goes, each in their own way, in their own time, would lean into me and infuse my soul with love beyond definition. They taught me to truly see without appearances clouding my sight, to hear what they communicated though their words were nearly silent, to simply accept the love they offered me without judgment or expectation.

⌒

I now realize that we are not separate outside of our individual bodies. Yet, I still revert to my feelings of suffering and separation when I first notice dying is in process. And I still grieve when a companion dies. I am the first to admit that I find it difficult to release that beautiful earthly form, the body! But in order to be helpful, I also realize that I must return to that perfect inner nature that ties all beings together. To be present for the dying and the transformation I must center and calm myself. And from that place of incredible peace, I can move back outward and support the transition.

In all respects I have, through time and experience, translated that first sense of respect and compassion for my little tree to all life around me. My hemlock tree, Corky, Jeffrey, even the ladybugs in October, and countless others throughout the years have stimulated in me a strong sense of commitment to be as fully present as I can be. With every creature I encounter, from the spider in the corner of my kitchen to my seventeen-year old goat, I take the time to focus, consider the sacred "Self," its true nature, our common ground. Then I am assured that I have found the best solutions, and can act with compassion.

Through challenging experiences I have found that becoming familiar with one's inner, true nature, that place of peace and connectedness to all life, is not a fast and easy trip. There are no instant techniques, no shortcuts. The most successful and enduring means that I have discovered for touching that nature is through a consistent meditation/contemplation practice to listen to my inner wisdom. Sometimes I only have time for five minutes of meditation or contemplation. Even in that short time I am usually able to gain insight. I have found that all the struggles and successes, the brief and sometimes even sustained glimpses of my true, inner nature, have been worth the effort.

When I first experienced an ability to enter that peaceful center and from there, meet and assist another, I finally began to understand who I am, why I am here, and the importance of helping those who are suffering. It is difficult to put such realization into words and I understand that each person's experience is a personal one. However, I have never regretted my commitment to this work based on compassion and loving kindness.

EIGHT

The Power of Prayer

When the animals first began coming to me many years ago for their healing through life and death, I was guided in my work by my great love for all beings. This work was reinforced by my own angels who communicated with me following the death of my mother's dog, Domino. Often, despite myself, I found myself doing things of a mystical, healing nature that I never would have thought of prior to Domino's passing. My desire to help the animals, especially those who were dying, spilled into my daily work with the animals in my care, as well as with people who were going through the illness or loss of their animal companions.

But I began to recognize that one of the more difficult aspects of working with a dying animal is the feeling of doing it alone without the support and encouragement of someone beside me, someone to cheer me on, as my grandmother used to say. As Michael and Tim became more involved with school and friends, and Doug's job kept him away from home longer hours, I became increasingly responsible for the daily care of the animals. This was also true when one of the animals was dying. At such times I had to learn to call on my inner resources, especially my angelic friends, to walk through particularly difficult situations. However, one of my greatest teachers for trusting my inner resources, turned out to be a duck.

Bart was a magnificent Khaki Campbell with striking brown and green feathers. Bart had an eternally youthful appearance, even when he reached the venerable age of twelve. Over his lifetime he had survived a weasel attack and a dog attack, escaping both without a single ruffled feather. He and his lady friend, Susan, a sweet black-and-white duck, would spend their days cruising the lawn for bugs, swimming in their personal pond, or napping in the shade. They were never apart from one another. As Bart aged, I worried that when he died Susan would follow in her grief for him since ducks mate for life. The thought of losing them both was unbearable.

One December day Bart staggered going up the steps to his nighttime pen. He seemed disoriented and wasn't really hungry. The next day at the animal hospital, I was told he was seriously anemic. "Probably bone marrow cancer," Dr. Partridge said. There was no cure. Bart's blood was boosted with iron, and he returned home to his beloved Susan.

Bart's red cell count rose, but I knew we were patching a sinking ship. With expediency, I felt compelled to sit down with both ducks and hold a conference. It was the first time I had tried such a meeting and I was surprised with the way the idea had flowed forth, as if it was the most natural thing to do. It seemed like nobody was listening, especially Bart and Susan, and I wasn't aware of any input from the angelic side of the "table." Yet, it felt appropriate and so I continued. I asked Bart to give me signs as to what he wanted to do, and when. After all, it was his life. Maybe it was just time. Perhaps Bart had chosen to leave. Who was I to argue if that was the case?

To Susan, my statements were a bit more inflexible. I wanted her to know that she was important to me, and that while she would miss Bart after he died, she did not have to leave. I reassured her that we would protect her, be her family and flock, and she would never be alone. And to my friends of the light, I prayed for guidance, courage, strength, clarity, peace of mind, and the wisdom to know how to help

Bart through his impending departure. I thanked them in advance, closed the meeting, passed around refreshments of corn and grapes, and left Bart and Susan to contemplate the moment.

What actually occurred in the meeting between Bart, Susan, myself, and the angelic beings was, in effect, prayer in action, or the interblending of physical and ethereal. There is a lightness and peace that comes over me whenever I am saying a truly heartfelt prayer as I did with Bart and Susan. It feels as if my body is dissolving into softness and luminosity. Science now knows that all cells have intelligence and respond positively or negatively to the messages they receive. Mind/body medicine stresses that thoughts create and alter one's physical reality in dramatic as well as subtle ways. Thus, one *becomes* anger, *becomes* peace, and *becomes* the prayers one forms.

There is considerable research today regarding the positive effects of prayer on health and well being. Drs. Larry Dossey and Bernie Siegel have excellent material available regarding these subjects. (See Resources for specific titles.) In essence, thought and word, when organized and projected outward, especially prayer, become powerful tools for those who seek to be a positive force in the world. When I work with animals, I tend to compose my own prayers relative to specific situations. These are usually inspired by the creature and the circumstance. Also, I ask for guidance from my angelic friends. With Bart and Susan, I combined prayer with creative visualization. This was my way of building a bridge between us so our communication could flow, and I could prepare for Bart's impending death.

Bart's anemia became increasingly difficult to shore up until one particular day in February, when we were scheduled to return to the vet hospital for yet another iron shot, Bart let me know unequivocally that he was preparing to die. I realized he had been paying attention at our meeting after all! I believe that because I had held that meeting, not only was I able to better read Bart's signals, I was also more prepared to respond in a helpful manner rather than if I had simply allowed myself to fumble through all those previous weeks.

I trusted that my angelic guides were close at hand, helping both Bart and me. Yet, my rational mind questioned what would be the best action to take. And so I hesitated as I put Bart in the car. Was he in pain? Would his suffering be prolonged unnecessarily if I kept him at home? Did he want to die at home in his familiar surroundings, near Susan and the others? Or should I take him to the animal hospital to be euthanized for a quick release? As usual, I was busy worrying the situation into chaos when I remembered my angelic friends. A few deep breaths, a quick moment of recognition, and I felt the connection with them come into focus. I asked for whatever help they were willing and able to give, recognizing that I could not ask them to interfere with Bart's own work without his permission. And then as much as possible, I silenced my mind.

My friend, Ellen, who was to ride over the mountain to the vet's with me, waited quietly while I eased Bart out of his carrier and placed him in a sunny place on the front lawn. I tried to remain connected to my angelic friends as I watched my feathered companion withdraw into himself, and distance himself from the outside world. All of Bart's energy and efforts were channeling within himself now, and it seemed he might be experiencing pain as the separation of soul and body accelerated. Another's suffering is always difficult for me to witness and with Bart, I leaned on my unseen helpers to ease his way, and mine.

Within minutes, Bart's eyes cleared and the pain dissipated. With the grace of a dancer, he simultaneously stretched his neck out and up. His bill rose into the air while he unfolded his wings and spread them to their maximum extension. Then his tail fanned out and for just a second, he held that position. Ellen and I could hardly breathe for the beauty of his movements. Then, with as much deliberation and poise, he closed his tail feathers, re-folded his wings to his body, and his head eased back to the ground. Bart was gone, his soul dancing somewhere in a realm where suffering and pain do not exist. For both Ellen and myself, Bart's death was the most beautiful one we had ever experienced, and one we would talk about with other people repeatedly.

Without my angelic guardians I could not have been so helpful. Ellen, too, was an indispensable support for me. After Bart's passage, we talked about our early concerns for his suffering, what we had each observed, how we were enriched, and the grief that both Susan, the duck, and I would soon be feeling.

While Susan had to decide to stay with us, or follow Bart, I couldn't help repeating to her my desire to have her stay. I had to trust that this time, my prayers would encourage healing of the highest order. As of this writing, four years after Bart's death, Susan is still with us. However, the first week after Bart's death I had my doubts that she would choose to stay, remembering Steffie and Little Eddie. I was very stern with Susan. I told her that even though I was being selfish, I needed her to remain with us, her family and flock who love her so much. And she obliged! I have no doubt that Bart is not too far way, keeping an eye on his beloved Susan with the angelic beings.

⌐ ·

Whether I view the passing of my animal friend as an immediate (or ultimate) blessing or not, has tremendous consequence when the actual process of transition is apparent. Choosing to wade right in and gather that warm body and soul close to me and comfort him or her in the dying process usually takes tremendous courage. What makes this easier is my belief that my actions, thoughts, and prayers reverberate into all the depths of life. They reach beyond the five senses of our physical reality and touch every aspect of body, mind, heart, and soul.

So when I pray, I become that prayer through my touch, voice, emotions, thoughts, and intentions. When I smooth fur or feathers or simply lay my hand just above the head, I pray, not for a cure, but for a healing. As with most animals who are dying, my prayers for Bart sounded like the following:

May Bart receive the healing he needs. Help him to come into full awareness, with peace and ease, free of fear and suffering.

Help me find the inner strength, courage, and peace to do this work. Remind me that I am an instrument for healing that will flow through me.

May joy, understanding, and resolution be present. May Bart heal into the fullness of life, or into the light of Spirit. If death is the final healing, may this be achieved without pain. Let his passage into death and beyond be easy and comforting to him.

After I offer prayers, I then envision the creature and myself embraced by Spirit to be protected and guided. Prayer of this nature supports all involved, whether it is the animal, a veterinarian (especially if euthanasia is appropriate), those beings of light, and myself.

With prayer, as with all methods of healing, I follow the old stand-by — to simply love and release. I do not believe lengthy or elaborate ritual is necessary to pray. Nor does one have to pray in a formal place of worship. Positive imaging or visualization, as part of prayer is vital, as it sets my highest intention into motion. It also helps me to soften to another's call for assistance.

I would like to offer three prayers that I have written and used in countless situations. I encourage all who care for animals and find themselves in critical situations with them, to form their own prayers as they come directly from the heart. Improvisation based on inspiration and love, rather than fear and chaos, is one of the kindest prayers one can give another.

The first prayer I wrote, called "The Aquarian Testament," takes the "Prayer of Saint Francis" in a slightly different direction. Rather than asking a higher power to *make* me into an instrument of peace, love, healing, etcetera, I am acknowledging and presenting to others that in my true nature, I am already unified with that powerful expression of love and compassion. In essence, I am an instrument ready and willing to act on my purest intentions. This prayer helps remove judgment of another's situation and allows for change and healing. "The Aquarian Testament" adapts easily to creative imagery and practiced on a regular basis provides a powerful exercise for strengthening and healing.

None of the following prayers are addressed to a specific deity, but to the one who is in crisis, acknowledging the true nature within that being. My prayer for, or to, another forms in my heart-center and is sent, encased in love, to his or her heart-center. I always leave time for any response that may be returned by the animal to me. I call this "Commune-ication," a process of speaking with and listening to one another, based on the sacred, common ground we share. And that, of course, is love, a cosmic language unto itself.

THE AQUARIAN TESTAMENT

When you come to me, know that we are both the Essence of God.
I will welcome you with honor, gratitude, and love.

And if you bring me anger, may I give you love;
If you bring fear, may I give you courage.
If you bring sorrow, may I give you joy;
If you bring uncertainty and doubt, may I give you peace.
And if you come willing to receive,
May I give you all that I am.

When you come to me,
I will see you and know you to be who you truly are,
Perfect in every way,
Always.

May all healing between us
Begin in the endless heart, yours, mine and that of all life,
Now and forever.

Namaste*

* Sanskrit: *I honor the place in you where we are one.*

As long as I understand that I have the ability to give love, courage, joy, honor, and peace *because I am these qualities or aspects*, (as are all beings) I will be able to choose these qualities rather than qualities I may not want such as anger, fear, sorrow, or doubt.

So I believe prayer functions as a means of asking for and giving assistance. Prayer is a declaration of my own greater purpose and ability. It is all that I am able to offer to others by way of service. Prayer is also a way for me to listen to that greatness within myself that I think of as my "true nature." This divine presence guides me through the dying process.

While prayer also serves as a statement of healing for another, I must take into account that greatness in others, allowing them their own choices around living and dying. Another favorite prayer I composed that addresses such a healing is as follows:

BEING OF LIGHT, FRIEND OF MY HEART

May you now receive all of the healing you desire,
blending into perfection within the rays of holiness,
expanding, softening, releasing all attachment, all resistance,
that now and from now forward
you are well in every aspect of your mind, body, heart, and soul.

May I, as your friend,
support your journey and your choices;
may I offer you courage, strength, peace, and love.
May the sacred light of your true nature
cleanse, purify, heal, and sustain you
from this moment on and forever more.

Namaste

When praying, there is strength in numbers. Whenever a critical situation arises at my sanctuary with one of the animals, I immediately contact certain friends and ask for their thoughts and prayers on the situation. It's comforting to know they're part of the process.

The last prayer offered here is another favorite. Its simplicity and directness make it a wonderful mantra that can be sung, chanted, or said repeatedly until a sense of peace and calm are evoked.

PRAYER FOR DYING

Beloved Friend:
I, with you,
resist nothing,
move in peace,
blessing this bridge.

Spirit we are:
unified always,
souls bonded
through our love;
now we are free.

Namaste

NINE

Communicating Without Words

The most accurate exchange between myself and an animal, or with my guides, often occurs when I can silence and empty my mind from daily concerns. Once I've done that, I gather my thoughts about what I want to communicate, carefully form and focus them in silence, and then project them to the animal or guide with whom I am working. When I feel I have received a response, I take appropriate action.

However, to silence and to empty the mind is difficult for humans, especially when tired. We tend to chatter endlessly, often too lost in deciding what to say next to hear any response. And because humans communicate with one another through sounds, we often instinctively anticipate an animal will respond in audible words. I have found that creatures and other beings of nature do most of their conversing mind-to-mind, adding body language and sounds for emphasis. Their telepathic communication is swift and subtle, usually undetected by the average person. When I am quiet, both in my thoughts and spoken words, I can then usually receive what the animals offer since they generally respond quite rapidly through thought, image, or colors.

In order for me to quiet my mind, I usually have to remind myself that when one thought stops, there is a gap, often so brief it is missed, before another thought begins to form. Because it is difficult to visualize a gap, I practice silence by visualizing a Japanese garden. When creating their gardens, the Japanese give careful consideration to the stones themselves, and their placement, conscious of the individual pieces and their relationship to the whole. It is the space between the stones they meditate on, rather than on the stones or other garden objects. So, once I have mindfully created and projected my thought, I try to be still in that space between the words. Then the answers flow back to me.

Of all the animals in my care, Sam is the one whom I most clearly hear. Sam can pierce my thoughts and words, and he consistently indicates that he has heard — and understood — everything I projected, mentally or verbally. Not that he always complies with my wishes! Sometimes people forget that animals are not mindless robots, but do have consciousness and decision-making abilities. They, too, create with their thought, even when under the dictates of a not-so-loving person.

According to a neighbor, Sam had been severely abused by his previous people who did not live far from our home. Apparently Sam had been frequently beaten and kicked. When he was about five-months old, Michael, Tim, and I found him thrashing around in the underbrush behind our property. He cried loudly, obviously in distress. Tim waded through poison ivy and blackberry brambles and when he emerged, Tim was carrying a dog in a terrible plight. Somehow, the pup had gotten his head into an old, very large, plastic jug and he couldn't get out of it. We removed the jug and set the pup near the fence, assuming he would run back to his home. Instead, he cowered and peered at us with terrified eyes. Phone calls around the neighborhood revealed his current situation. I named him Sam and vowed he would never be returned to his former home.

For the past thirteen years Sam has remained an honored member of our family. He has been shown only respect and appreciation, even for his often aggressive ways as he rules his pack as alpha-dog. And sometimes Sam truly believes he knows best, even though I might disagree.

When Sam was about two and still full of fear and uncertainty, I had to take a job away from home for several hours a day. Left on his own, Sam panicked. Each day I would return to find sofa or chair cushions shredded, kitchen cabinets wide open with food spilled everywhere, and magazines torn into tiny pieces. Being so tired, my impulse was to be angry, but I also realized his predicament. Because he had bonded primarily with me, he had become completely dependent on me for his physical and emotional welfare. When I left, Sam was terrified I would not return. I began working with him.

Each morning before leaving, I would sit next to Sam, tell him I was leaving, but that I would return at the end of the day. I would send him a mental picture of myself walking in through the door. Then I gave Sam a job to show my confidence in him. I asked him to be Housekeeper. He didn't have to vacuum, I told him, but if he would see that everything stayed in its place, he would receive a Housekeeper Treat when I returned. From the first time that I went through this type of communication with him, he never again disturbed anything in the house, and hasn't since.

In all types of communication, verbal or silent, I am reminded by the animals that I am responsible for the kind of message I project, and its intention. I am careful to communicate through understanding, support, encouragement, love, and respect. In Sam's case, I needed to reassure him that he was safe and secure at home and that I would be back at the end of the day.

Not long after that, Sam began jumping out of the enclosed dogs' garden whenever he was let outside. Because we live close to a road, I was concerned for his safety, and asked him again and again to remain in the fence. Sam chose to follow his own thoughts on the matter and jumped the fence the minute I was on the other side.

One morning I tried to catch him, but he kept skittering just out of reach. I sat on the grass and he sat on the grass, looking the other way. He knew my frustration. I was thinking to myself, *Why does he keep jumping out when I've asked him not to?* Instantly, a clear thought shot through my head: *Because I want to be with you.* That simple, that direct. Sam was, by now, looking straight through me.

So I offered Sam a deal. He could come out with me in the early mornings while I fed the large animals, only if he would agree to stay within the fence at all other times. I did not receive a positive response from him. In fact, I believe he chose to be silent on the matter. But the next morning I upheld my end of the bargain and Sam has not jumped over the fence in the ten years since my deal.

Many of the animals in my care have shown me that animals read and respond to human thoughts and intentions, rather than verbalizations. So if I say one thing, but think another, it is the *thought* that the animal takes to heart, acts upon, or withdraws from. Which brings us back around to the importance of expectations I hold regarding an animal's healing, especially if those expectations are highly charged emotionally. If a dying animal is a long-standing friend, she may attempt to react in compliance with my feelings. For example, if I am verbally telling my old dying dog to let go of her body, but my grief is causing my mind to wish she wouldn't die, more than likely she will try to hang on as long as possible. This confusion opens the way for more pain and suffering and added grief for both of us.

When I communicate with a dying animal, it is imperative that I am sensitive to the creature's extremely vulnerable position, possibly in pain, frightened, certainly weak and susceptible to *my* fears, grief, and frustration. I have developed a whole new language that is based on impulse, feeling, intuition, and plain old gut reaction rather than words and sounds. And always, I communicate with love and honor, and in a nonjudgmental manner.

For communication to be helpful, I have had to recognize within myself and the animals the point of commonality, or communion, through which we may communicate. When one is suffering, that is not the time to criticize or to plead for that being not to die. Nor is it appropriate to attempt to persuade another that I am smarter and know better what it is they need. When an animal is dying, that is the time to offer only *releasing* love, appreciation, and respect. I don't need to take charge and run things my way. Who's dying here anyway? I need to step to one side, keep pace with the dying one, and listen, observe, and respect the choices of that individual.

Death does not always come rapidly. Nor is it often clear, at first, that an animal has begun dying. I will speak more on this later, but for now I want to emphasize that illness or disability, even if considered so-called "terminal" by the medical profession, does not mean that the animal should be rushed to the vet's office for euthanizing. The animal may still want to be a part of life. While a deteriorating physical condition may require increasing work on my part, and certainly a balance of mind and emotions, I have learned that the animals will tell me when they are ready to be helped on. Or they may choose to die in their own way, in their own time.

Waggy is an excellent example of what I mean. The last few months of his life were especially difficult for me. Often I just wanted the whole experience to end, even though I didn't want Waggy to die before her time, and I knew I would miss her terribly after she was gone. And I worried about her suffering. No one needs to suffer — I do not believe that it is a prerequisite for learning on any level. Yet, by listening carefully to Waggy, and continually asking her to let me know when she had had enough, I was able to clearly understand her when on that Tuesday morning before Thanksgiving, she was ready to be released. And I didn't hesitate.

Another one of my teachers in the art of interspecies communication was a ferocious little rabbit whom I called Benny The Bruiser. He spent his days driving the other rabbits in the warren into corners and beating the stuffing out of them. The first bunnies, barely old enough to leave their mothers, had been adopted by Michael and Tim from the Albemarle County Fair. In time, and quite by our negligence, they produced several more, who all grew into happy healthy rabbits housed in a specially designed pen. But every group has its bully, and Benny was the one.

One day I found Benny flat on the ground beside one of the rabbit houses. A trip to the vet revealed a severe middle ear infection that, in rabbits, is unable to be corrected. For whatever life he had remaining, Benny would have "head-tilt," a medical condition in which his head lies flat over to the side, while the rest of his body was in its normal upright position.

The head-tilt meant that Benny could no longer function on his own in the rabbit pen. He was moved inside to our house "crate," a wire enclosure in a bright area with lots of fresh air. His crate was covered in soft towels to protect the side of his face next to the ground. Three times a day we changed and cleaned his towels, and we carefully supported his head as he ate and drank. Benny received the best of treats: carrots, lettuce, mint (a rabbit favorite), and other delights.

Dr. Partridge thought he would die fairly soon, but Benny surprised us all and continued to thrive in his new environment. Everyone in the family held Benny frequently, gave him extra hugs, and praised him for his courage. While at first he fought us and seemed angry at his situation, quickly Benny began to show a change of heart. Rather, he began to show heart! Soon, he snuggled close when we held him, and licked our hands, instead of trying to nip at them. In time he gained a new nickname: Benny The Beneficent.

As was my tradition, I gave Benny the standard talk: "You'll have to let me know when you've had enough of this; if you want help journeying on, be clear; or if you want to die at home, let me know. I'm here for the long haul."

Sure enough, one morning in April, nearly a year after he first developed head-tilt, Benny let me know without question that the time had come for him to die and continue his journey. With no effort at all, he raised his head to look at me, an impossible task for all the time he had suffered head-tilt. Now he had something to communicate and I got it right away. I took him out of his enclosure and held him in a soft towel, encouraging him one last time as he died, naturally and softly. "King Benny" I called him then, the bravest of rabbits anywhere. He had experienced many things in his brief lifetime, grown immeasurably through a most difficult lesson in the past year, and graduated with honors.

And if I had had him euthanized when he was first diagnosed? What we all would have missed! Especially Benny.

⌒

Mindfulness is a wonderful term that is often used in Buddhist philosophy to describe the bringing of one's awareness to the fullness of the present moment. Many times while washing dishes or cleaning stalls my fractured mind races from one thought to another, worrying about possible future situations, agonizing over an error the day before, or anticipating disaster. But when I focus on the task — the sensation of water on my hands, the sound of the dishes as they touch one another, the song of birds and insects when I am in the barn, or the gentle nuzzling of the donkeys and goats against my arm as I clean — this brings my tortured mind back into the present. Mindfulness of the task at hand allows my mind to rest in the moment, and be at peace.

Over the years, through the help of wise teachers both human and animal, I have discovered the importance of participating as fully as possible in everything I do. Granted, I continually use every method of meditation I have learned to accomplish this! For example, instead of doing three things at once, I try to finish one task at a time, giving my full attention, and being alert to every aspect, including listening to inner guidance regarding that task. This is especially true when an animal goes into life and death crisis. Then I *must* slow down, try not to get distracted by the phone or demands of others unless they are equally as critical. I especially have to watch that I do not get caught up in my own relentless negative emotions of helplessness, fear, frustration, and grief.

One way I find effective for slowing down and focusing my attention is to be aware of my breathing. When I feel a rush of fear or frustration, I become as still as possible and breathe in deeply, then breathe out fully. I focus on the sensation of my breath leaving my mouth as if I am letting out a deep sigh of contentment. Sometimes I visualize the in breath as pure light and the out breath as cloudy and gray, representing all the negative stuff leaving. I continue until I sense the out breath to be just as clear as the in breath. At the same time I remind myself that breath is *prana*, the energy of life shared by all on Earth. This allows me to relax and push back those negative borders until I feel more capable of continuing the work in a positive frame of mind.

Another powerful method for gathering focus and calming an anxious mind is to have on hand a picture or other image of someone who inspires me. I have a statue of Buddha, inherited from my mother who, in turn, kept it close to her for several decades. I also have a reproduction of a painting called *The Compassionate Christ*, which shows a radiant Christ with animals of all kinds gathering at his feet, resting in his open, outstretched hands, and a squirrel on one shoulder, and a small bird on the other. These spiritual masters remind me of my purpose, my *greater* purpose for being here — to help all beings through my thoughts, words, and actions.

Prayer, already touched on in an earlier chapter, likewise helps me to focus and return fully to the present situation. For me, there are few things more encouraging than conversation with my angels, knowing they are surrounding the animals and myself, always ready to assist.

Please understand that I am not suggesting that you suppress negative emotions and feelings, or try to cover them up with so-called positive affirmations. When I feel negative emotions I sit quietly with those emotions, and watch them with as much detachment as possible, using any of the methods given above. Before long, my negative feelings will begin to dissolve on their own. I must remind myself that I am not my emotions, but simply the observer, the witness. Emotions are as natural as breathing, but I do not need to hold onto them, or become them.

When anger, fear, frustration, or grief arise, I gently remind myself that being human means having such feelings. They are not "bad," nor am I a "bad" person for experiencing them. All of my emotions are a vital part of my own growth and awakening. By observing my emotions, I am able to discern between those states that leave me exhausted and scattered, and my true nature, which offers me peace and a sense of harmony. So when those negative states occur, as they will, I acknowledge them and watch them. I let them drift and change and dissolve. When a negative emotion arises, I try to study it in a detached manner, instead of saying, *I am angry* or *I am fearful.* It always amazes me how the emotion begins to evaporate until it disappears altogether.

Hannah was one of those animals who taught me the importance of being in each moment, attentive to the impermanence of life. A beautiful dog with long, slender legs, Hannah loved running hard and fast, more than anything except for eating. When she was nearly eleven years old, she began to develop degenerative myelopathy, a disease of the spine in which the myelin sheath that covers the nerves along the spinal column, disintegrates. The result for Hannah was increasing loss of use of her muscles, nerves, and legs from mid-back to tail. For Hannah, it appeared to be tragic and I longed for her to be able to run again. Yet, with each stage of the disease, she expressed no complaint, adjusting smoothly to each change in her condition. Through her own grace and acceptance of her condition, Hannah taught me how to live each stage of life.

Caring for Hannah required that I constantly be mindful of her needs as they changed. For many months she was still able to walk and run through our woods each day, propelling herself along by her front feet at a great speed while I held her up by her tail, hanging on for the ride. When she no longer showed an interest in such adventures, I helped her outside to sit on the lawn and watch the fields and mountains across from us. Then the colder days of fall arrived and such outings were uncomfortable for her. From then on, she stayed on her special bed by the heater, still enjoying all the activities of our human and animal family, appreciating her meals and treats, protective of her space.

Hannah was not ready to die for several weeks after she reached this stage. While no longer able to run and dig, she still seemed to have a peace that radiated from her whole body. I was enriched simply by sitting with her, stroking her soft brown coat. I still did not sense that she was preparing to die; she seemed to be integrating and experiencing life to the best of her physical ability.

Like so many of the creatures in my care over the years, Hannah outdistanced the projected diagnosis of Dr. Partridge by nearly a year. As a large, eighty-pound dog she was already considered "old" at twelve, yet she did not show some of the typical evidence of aging such as slower attention, increased sleeping, or a graying muzzle. Hannah, as with so many I have known, progressed at her own unique rate.

Impermanence taught me that her situation could change at any moment. On a bright November day, Hannah let me know it was her time to die. She had had a disturbed night, barking constantly, and chewing on her bedding. I knew she was uncomfortable, but as she ate a normal breakfast, I questioned what she was trying to tell me. I sat next to her and took her head in my lap. Again I repeated the now well-rehearsed talk about helping her on if that was what she wanted. Then, I asked her directly, *Do you want to die?* Immediately, she wagged her tail. As with Benny lifting his head, considering Hannah's paraplegic condition, wagging her tail ought to have been impossible. Then, as if to emphasize her desire, she reached up and licked me on the nose. I knew it was time. Several hours after Dr. Partridge had helped her die, I realized what she had been telling me by licking my nose: *Yes, Rita, you got my message — you were right on the nose!*

When I am mindful, I appreciate living here on Earth, in this body, with this creature, in this situation, alert and present to what is needed of me. If I could give any gift to a friend who is living, or who is dying, it would be an appreciation for each moment.

TEN

A Hand to Hold,
a Soul to Ease

My mother got sick again in the spring of 1997. My sister, Sylvia, whom I call Tao, had come from Maine to take care of our mother for a week and had brought her aged dog, Honey, with her. Honey was close to dying, but Tao still thought it could be awhile, but not likely. Towards the end of my sister's first week at Mom's, Tao decided to stay longer. Five days later, on Sunday, Honey died in the night.

Tao called me Monday morning to let me know. I told her one of my elderly goats, Isabelle, likewise, seemed to be dying. I was not surprised as she would be sixteen soon. We talked a long time on the phone that day, about life and death, suffering and aging. Our mother, then eighty-four, had wanted to die for a long time and was physically in decline.

After I hung up the phone, I made the decision to ease Isabelle on her way. Since my sister wanted to have Honey's body cremated before she returned home, we decided to go together over that mountain I so often traveled to the Woodworth Animal Hospital. We lifted Isabelle into the back of my Subaru wagon and placed Honey's body on the front seat. My sister had put Honey's body into an old wicker laundry basket, wrapped in a beautiful blanket, flowers and herbs tucked here and there. Tao rode in the back so she could hold Isabelle's head steady on our bumpy, winding road and calm her. I concentrated on driving through rain and fog. We were, as my sister has noted several times, a team.

At the animal hospital, Dr. Dan, in his usual friendly, compassionate manner, helped us with both our beloveds. Perhaps Honey's soul, already gone on, was with us to encourage Isabelle in her departure. Overall, it was a memorable event, despite our sorrow.

Afterwards we had lunch at a small restaurant, comforting one another over the loss of two special friends. Over our meal we paid tribute to Honey and Isabelle by remembering the lives they so generously shared with us, their companions and caregivers. We raised our cups of coffee to their renewed journey, wished them well, and thanked them for all they had given us.

Home again, exhausted, I sat in the barn, comforting grieving Emily, Isabelle's twin sister and last member of our original herd. Tao went back to Mom's. But distance and hours did not break our connection. Even now we speak of that shared time, an experience that would have been substantially diminished had the other sister-with-creature not been there. It was, of course, another facet to my education by the animals regarding death, and how to make it a conscious, merciful event not only for the one passing, but for myself as a participant.

I am always grateful for those willing to be with me as I sit with a dying animal companion. Perhaps they make me a hot cup of tea or coffee, or join with me in chants and prayers as we build sacred space around us. It makes a tremendous difference when I have someone with whom to cry, a nonjudging ear to listen to my concerns and fears, a hand to hold, arms around me, silliness at critical points to break the tension. These are all essential aspects of a support team for caregivers. For years I had wanted to create a hospice program for animals and their families. A major event in my own family in the fall of 1998 made me aware of another aspect of dying that calls strongly for a hospice program for animals to be established.

The experience with Tao, Honey, and Isabelle just six months earlier, became an initiation into the far more intense work I would be doing with my own mother's dying. A part of me dreaded going through this inevitable and impending experience.

Almost from the day my mother arrived at my home in October, she showed marked, growing weakness, a frailty that had not been there in the previous months. Most disturbing to me were signs of what her doctor termed dementia. Intuitively I felt that she had come home to die. She certainly wanted to die, feeling she was no longer of any use since her stroke four years prior, followed by a heart attack, a weakened back, and lost eyesight. Getting her out of bed was torture, for both of us, but I pressed her on it, by doctor's orders, so that she would perhaps regain some of the strength that was fast leaving her.

Nights at our home were horrendous. Often she would have nightmares or be awake and delusional, thrashing in her bed, first hot, then unbearably cold, or unable to breathe. She became increasingly difficult to handle and cruel in what she said to me. Once she threw her pillow at me, another time she threw her medicine. She even told me I was the cause of her pain and decline. By Christmas that year I knew my mother was obviously dying.

Until my mother was admitted to the hospice unit at the hospital in early January 1998, I was confused regarding the actual closeness of her death. But as she proceeded through the dying process, I was able to draw on the support and expertise of the attending staff. During that time I had several profound insights regarding not only my mother's personal passage, but that of others, including animals.

In many ways, my mother's dying was a remarkable event. For the first time since I had begun sitting with dying animals, I was able to witness that process with someone, in this case my mother, who could verbalize what she was experiencing. Ananda, one of the hospice nurses and a practicing Sufi, helped me understand better than anyone else what was happening to my mother.

Over the previous three months, my mother had begun exhibiting cycles of clarity and so-called "normal" behavior, interspersed with brief bouts of dementia, or "abnormal" behavior during which times she seemed immersed in other worlds, and even dimensions. While she was still living with me, her doctor wanted to medicate her with anti-psychotic drugs. I refused his prescriptions, sensing that quite possibly she was crossing in and out of her body. I wondered if during these "abnormal" times she was becoming more accustomed to life beyond the physical world. Intuitively, I felt I should not interfere, even though increasingly so, her "abnormal" behavior became bizarre and unpredictable.

Once in hospice, Ananda and another nurse, who is a practicing Buddhist, explained that, yes, in fact my mother was indeed going through a most wonderful and necessary process of experiencing the "other side" as well as letting go of subconscious baggage that had plagued her all her life. "Like peeling away the layers of an onion," Ananda explained. As I sat with my mother, now rarely fully conscious for any length of time, I watched her cycles come at almost perfect fifteen-second intervals. First, she would twist back and forth on the pillow, her left arm flailing in the air as she mumbled proclamations of past events and people with which I was familiar and could identify. My sister, Tao, the nurses, and I would hold her hands, and tell her we loved her. We reassured my mother that she was safe and could let go of whatever it was that was distressing her. Then, she would begin to quiet, say to the best of her ability, "Okay," and then drift into a fifteen-second cycle of apparent sleep. I describe her sleep as "apparent" only because we felt she was actually leaving her body at such times.

As her hospital stay continued past a week, she spent more time in her sleeping states than in her distressed, semi-wakeful ones. Concurrently, the deep lines and furrows in my mother's face that she had had since her stroke, softened, and she began to appear lighter, younger, and so very beautiful. When the difficult cycles did arise for our mother again, Tao and I sat with her, reminding her of our presence and love, chanting and singing songs, and reading poetry to her. Again, we reassured her that we would be fine and that we would take care of each other. And she would quiet again.

My mother's final breath was a grace-filled release. She simply breathed out one last time, and was gone. Her face relaxed and she was at peace. At that moment of death, those of us standing by her felt her freedom.

During those long nights spent at the hospice unit, I had many helpful conversations with the nursing staff regarding the work I do with animals. Several were in agreement that nonhumans go through the same process that I was witnessing in my mother. For example, animals, especially dogs, can become irritable and even snappy in their elder years. People with such animals in their care have consistently told me that sadly, they felt the animal should be put to sleep. They were also concerned about the possibility of their animal being in chronic pain, and being uncomfortable with life in general, perhaps even a danger to people.

When my mother was spiteful, hurling her pillow at me — a strong departure from the person who had raised me to always be gentle, kind and compassionate—she would often then become sad, assuring me again and again how much she loved me. Knowing my mother's personality so well, I realize in retrospect that she was simply moving through a painful process of separation from those close to her, and doing so in the only way she knew. If such episodes had been the result of mini-strokes, she would not have been able to so quickly and clearly express her heartfelt love and appreciation for me.

There were two instances when I would have done anything to have been able to stop the panic and pain I saw course through my mother's body in the last three days of her life. Had she been one of the animals in my care, I would have strongly considered euthanasia. Of course, this was not possible, and for that I am now grateful. Her spells lasted only a few moments, relieved by carefully dosed morphine and the supportive work of her daughters and the nurses. And each time my mother passed through those terrible moments, she moved to a fuller level of peace. I believe those two particular instances pushed her through final blocks that allowed her to eventually let go and step from this life a free and easy soul.

In a rapidly growing global consciousness that opens the human heart to embrace all beings as sacred, it is imperative to recognize and support not only the physical mechanisms of life and death, but the expansive workings and evolution of the soul/spirit within all living beings. It is no longer adequate to say, "My dog is old, arthritic, increasingly grumpy, even paraplegic, therefore his quality of life is diminished and he should be put to sleep." To believe that these precious ones who bless our lives are more than just their physical bodies, as we now believe for ourselves, requires that we also be willing to assist the animal's *soul* on its full and eternal journey.

Such work requires mindfulness, detachment, and a willingness to listen to, and support what the creature wants, physically and soul-wise. Each case is unique, calling on different resources. Kidney failure, advanced heart disease, cancer, or trauma such as gunshot wounds or car accidents do not usually allow much time for the kind of dying experience my mother was able to have. But these situations can be worked with in another way, and be just as helpful.

Not for a moment am I advocating that people allow an animal to suffer prolonged bouts of pain and fear. But I now better understand the importance of the dying process, even the hard parts, and I know there are ways that animals can be supported and eased through it. Pain can be diminished by proper medication and the fear dissolved through certain methods described in the next chapter. Euthanasia certainly can be a blessing, and mindfulness and attention tell the caregiver when this is called for.

In all circumstances, a support program for animals in crisis and their families will provide reassurance that no matter what the final decisions, no matter the final outcome, those who stand by their dying companions will be enriched with caring faces, willing ears, and strong arms to comfort and encourage. And afterward, when the inevitable grief and questioning arise, a support group, much like hospice, can provide immeasurable comfort. Without my sister, the nurses, and the volunteers of the hospice unit, I could never have helped my mother as I did. Nor could I have eased Isabelle, the goat, through her passage, and my own grieving process as well if I had not had help. That is teamwork.

For animals, home hospice care is only just beginning to find acceptance. I believe hospice care for animals is a movement that will find rapid momentum in the years ahead. Recently, a friend remarked that one of her horses was not doing so well. "We're just doing hospice for her now," Ruth said. A sign of wonderful things to come.

ELEVEN

Tools for Caregivers

Snowstar was my gentle giant of the goat herd. Mostly white and gray with low-hanging Nubian ears, his quiet, soft ways made him a favorite with all who met him. He was a big goat, easily standing a foot taller at the shoulder than the females, but he never showed aggression, even towards the other males in the group.

As with most wethers (neutered male goats) who often do not live as long as female goats, Snowstar began to show problems when he reached the age of ten. Snowstar had never been sick up to that point, however I've learned that when a goat stops eating, *and* isn't chewing cud, I'd better get out the thermometer, pay attention to details, and have one hand on the phone to call the vet. And so I did with Snowstar.

First he stopped eating. Then his rumen became too quiet — none of the delightful gurgles and growls that indicate his multiple-chambered stomach is properly processing the food. Two missed meals, while not necessarily life-threatening, was cause for concern and so I began trying to bring Snowstar's system back into balance and raise his energy level. I noticed that he seemed cold, yet was not showing signs of an elevated temperature. The next step was to turn to some useful tools right at hand.

After reading various texts on healing with color and light I found through my own experimentation that different colors definitely have an effect on both an animal's physical and emotional condition. (See Resources for more information.) For example, the colors red and yellow generate physical energy when an animal is ill or generally weak. So I keep a soft yellow blanket on hand for such times. With Snowstar, I laid this blanket over his back while he rested. He began to relax, indicating that the yellow blanket brought him some comfort. If he had not wanted the blanket — some animals do not like to have anything over them — I would have rolled it up and placed it beside him, along his back, but on the ground. I was glad to see that no one in the herd was interested in dragging the blanket off or eating it!

Snowstar may have developed a malignant tumor somewhere in his digestive system, although in the beginning of his illness, there was no way to know this. Nonetheless, apparently it was time for him to move on because he began to develop a high fever and never did regain his appetite. Even antibiotics did not bring him around.

Three days into his illness I intuitively felt Snowstar prepare to die, even though Dr. Dan felt he might yet recover. His ears drooped that much lower, his eyes dulled, and he now seemed uncomfortable with the blanket. Because he still seemed cold from the fever, I switched to a white blanket, which has a peaceful affect as well as being a bit thicker for extra warmth. This one he accepted.

I sat with Snowstar into the night, encouraging him in his journey, reminding him that he was always safe and greatly loved. Finally, I told him I had to get some sleep and would see him in the morning. "If you die in the night," I told him, "I wish you a safe, easy passage." Then I called on the angels to watch over him, and went to bed. When I checked on Snowstar at 2 AM, he had died, apparently in peace. His head was folded back along his shoulder as goats will do when they sleep. I sat with his body for awhile, talking to his soul as I tucked the blanket around him.

Snowstar's easy death made me aware of an aspect of dying that is often ignored: other animals who are aware of the situation and their reaction. In this case, there were other goats in the herd. I have had other animals struggle through death, and the effect has been disturbing, especially in a group that by nature, is a family or herd. Even though I was not present when Snowstar died, I felt he had not suffered or fought the process by the way I found his body. In addition, the other goats seemed unconcerned, yet definitely aware as we removed his body. They clustered together and watched us. Once the stall was clear the herd returned to eating their hay and napping in the morning sun. It was evident that helping Snowstar through his passage, helped the rest of the herd as well. Perhaps the colored blankets affected the other goats in a positive way. Did they, too, receive energy from the yellow blanket and peace from the white blanket?

Tools, such as colored blankets, are useful and I make sure they are available at my sanctuary. However, my work with animals also requires *simplicity* in order to remain clear. Therefore, colored cloth and other tools that I use need to be easily acquired, and need little space to store. And the rituals I use such as singing, chanting or prayer, are not lengthy or involved. Once I begin to worry or fuss about whether I'm "doing it right" or become distressed because I have forgotten or lost something to ease a dying animal, then the tools cease to be useful. In the end, worrying about things I don't have at hand will only hinder the work. Truly, all one really needs to ease an animal through death is right in one's heart — love and a sense of expanded awareness. The most powerful tool of all is when holding a dying animal to consciously encourage and support release of that soul.

Even during the period following death, I try to be present. During this passage the soul may find itself in confusion and concern for the person left behind. That is why I sat with Snowstar's body and kept the white blanket over him even after he had died. I continued to assure him, wherever his soul was, that he was safe and loved. I knew that although his body was lifeless, his soul was very much alive. I tried to stay aware of the real possibility that Snowstar was present in the barn with me, separated only by my perception.

Waggy's reappearance a year after her death had convinced me of this possibility.

When an animal is dying, and even when the soul has left the body, I like to use different colors as well as music, sound, and flower essences. (See Resources.) There is nothing in any of these tools that is harmful or toxic to the caregiver or the creature. All are found in or represent nature, and except for the flower essences, are inexpensive to buy and keep on hand. While the flower essences are more costly, I have found from my own experience that they are invaluable. All three tools are a joy to use. They bring a special kind of peace and light into the situation.

COLORED CLOTH

Colored cotton cloth, such as the one I used with Snowstar, is an excellent way to comfort all animals, including chickens and ducks. Deep blue, white, and gold are the most useful when an animal has entered the initial stages of death. Animals may not necessarily see the colors; however, in my experience they respond dramatically to the *vibration* of light that translates to human eyes as color.

The easiest way to present these colors to an animal is through clean, natural fabric, preferably a soft cotton. Blue is the color of inner peace and calm and encourages surrender, or non-resistance. White encourages and strengthens the soul aspect of a being, and in the case of dying provides extra energy to the soul to help it move into its new ethereal aspect. Gold, likewise, seems to help strengthen and encourage the soul so that the crossing out of body is less stressful. Use colors that are as clear and as pure as possible, rather than gray-toned. Any of the blues are appropriate and the gold can range into the yellows and ochres.

I am also careful to dress in certain colors that will send healing vibrations. When our mother was dying in the hospital, my sister and I wore blues and purples, colors to soften her body's process and strengthen her soul's work. Purple was her favorite color. We knew that even though she was blind she would sense its vibration and be comforted.

I often go one step further and, after the death is complete, wrap the body in the same cloth and bury them together, unless, of course, the body is cremated. The color continues to support separation of physical body and soul, encouraging the soul in its own process.

In some cases, such as at the veterinarian's office for euthanasia, or when an animal has been killed on the road, use of cloth is not always possible. At such times I simply close my eyes and visualize the appropriate color surrounding the animal, knowing the thought is equally as powerful. In fact, this applies to any of the tools listed here. Death usually does not wait for the perfect setting, or preparation!

Music and Sound

The use of music and sound in healing is well documented relative to work with humans, and much of it is applicable to animals as well. My initiation into the affects of sound came in a most unusual way, through an unexpected and remarkable little creature.

Spiders come and go in our house, but mostly go. Webs are periodically wiped from doorjambs and swept from ceilings to keep our home "within standards." One black spider, however, cleverly built her nest in the corner of our kitchen window, smack over the hole used daily by a stream of ants. She was so industrious at ant control that I granted her asylum and named her Sara.

Over the summer and fall months the spider and I led separate lives, occasionally acknowledging each other's presence over the morning dishes. We kept our distances, neither being especially fond or trusting of the other. Over Thanksgiving's unwashed plates I noticed the nest firm, but dusty, had been abandoned.

"Died," I assumed. "Spiders do that this time of year. I wonder where her egg cases are?" I finished washing the last fork and reminded myself to clean away the nest in the morning. But I am not a punctual house cleaner and the web was neglected for the oncoming December holiday rush.

December: Cookie baking, candle lighting, and my favorite, Christmas music. As I stood washing dishes, I enthusiastically sang "We Three Kings," then rolled into "Oh Christmas Tree." I glanced to the windowsill to find Sara happily reinstated, two legs draped over the nest's rim, listening intently.

Silence. Sara retreated. Cautiously, I hummed the opening bars to "The First Noel," watching that nest as anxiously as if she had been the opera critic for *The New York Times*. Sure enough, over hooked one hairy leg, then another, another, another ...and up came her head with eight shining eyes.

Not to be outdone, I rushed to the tape player and put on Handel's "Messiah," charging back to the sink in time to give the "Hallelujah" chorus my full attention. By its conclusion, Sara perched on the edge of her nest, swaying back and forth, sighing (I would swear) as the London Philharmonic Choir and I extended the final exhilarating note.

Through experimentation I discovered Sara to have exquisite taste in music. My sons' rock-'n-roll sent her cringing to the furthest corner of her nest. Bach and Beethoven brought her back up, two or four furry legs draped comfortably over the topmost edge. Her favorite was always Johann Pachebel's "Canon in D Major," preferring pianist George Winston's version above all others. In this we were in perfect accord.

Such was the relationship Sara and I developed through our mutual love of music, that I began to look forward to washing dishes, often pausing on odd trips through the kitchen to discuss musical interpretation with my new friend. Although short on verbal replies, her tiny eyes sparkled appreciation and we became quite fond of each other. Music filled the often webby corners of the house, and trust melted the wall of doubt between us.

On Christmas Day I discovered that Sara was gone, her nest as hollow as the feeling inside me. "She came back before," I reasoned, "maybe in a few days ...." At every meal's conclusion I searched the windowsill, but the nest remained abandoned.

Died, I mourned. The house became silent. I sang less and disliked washing dishes immensely.

I should be grateful, I thought. Sara had stayed longer than most spiders even live and she had been an excellent teacher. I, the self-acclaimed animal appreciator who had so carelessly wiped off the spider kingdom as a household inconvenience, had at one time, even thought them insidious, ugly, and dangerous. But Sara gently reminded me how precious every life form is and that behind every quadruple set of eyes, within even the tiniest hairy body, lives a spark called Spirit.

I'll leave the nest another week, just in case …I hoped. I missed Sara a lot. I wondered if she missed me.

The second week of January, Pachebel's famous "Canon in D Major" rang through the sensitive fingers of George Winston, and warmed our home on a very cold day. I went to the kitchen to check the time, my intuition sensing the familiar soft black form before my eyes saw my beloved Sara meandering across the ceiling. She kept moving toward the window sill until her nest, full once again, reflected the joy in my heart.

From then on she left her nest frequently, setting off on secret journeys with destinations appropriate only for spiders. And each time when she returned to her windowsill home, she ate ants, and I washed dishes — both with great enthusiasm — and together we shared music, the bond between friends.

Like Sara, animals seem especially drawn to Baroque music, and since my experience with her, I have discovered the supportive power of chants of various cultures. Chants use repetitive words and syllables specifically created to invoke a healing that transcends physical curing, and seem to reach to the very essence, or soul of the individual. I am particularly fond of traditional Tibetan Buddhist chants, although they do take some getting used to. At first I did not care for them and felt almost uncomfortable. But a second listening, with full concentration, drew me, as if I was listening to the sound of the planets, especially Earth.

Mantras are a favorite to sing as I work around the animals, feeding, cleaning, or grooming. I originally discovered with Sara that singing mantras helps me to be present in the moment, generating an inner sense of peace and completeness. This in turn radiates out to the animals and all that surrounds me, making me aware of my connectedness to all things. Certainly, the animals enjoy it. Christina, my cow, is particularly appreciative, leaning into me in a sleepy manner so that much of her thousand-pound body needs support — quite an experience!

Other than Handel and Pachabel, I have a favorite chant learned long after Sara and I first discovered each other. This particular chant is called the *Prajnaparamita*, the Heart Sutra, a Buddhist text that in essence contains the heart of Buddha's teachings. This particular sutra, thousands of years old, is so essential to Buddhists for enlightenment, they recite or chant it on a daily basis. The core teaching of the Heart Sutra says that by recognizing that form is emptiness, and emptiness is form, one learns nonattachment and thus, freedom from suffering.

Emptiness here does not mean "nothingness," but basically, "All That Is," no separation, no definition. For me, studying and understanding the Heart Sutra has been very helpful in my work. The Heart Sutra brings me great insight for my death and dying work. It also brings me inner peace in many different situations. I recommend a small volume written by Vietnamese Zen master, Thich Nhat Hanh, called, *The Heart of Understanding, Commentaries on the Prajnaparamita Heart Sutra*. This book is easy and pleasant to read. The author carefully explains the meaning of the Heart Sutra. Thich Nhat Hanh also explains the accompanying mantra of *Avalokitesvara*, the Bodhisattva (awakened being) of Compassion, which is, in Sanskrit, as follows:

Gate, gate, paragate, parasamgate, bodhi, svaha.

Translated, this means, "Gone, gone, gone all the way over, everyone gone to enlightenment, (and) *svaha*: a cry of joy."

The vibration from this mantra strengthens and liberates me as the chanter as well as the one cared for. When my sister held Isabelle, the goat, in the back seat, she eased Isabelle's distress by chanting the Heart Sutra as we drove over the mountain and while Isabelle was being euthanized. It was remarkable to watch how chanting calmed Isabelle, as she peacefully stepped from her body. Tao and I also chanted this particular mantra for our mother throughout her time in the hospice unit. After she died, we chanted to help her as she crossed into the etheric realm.

About fifteen months after the experience with my mother's death I had another astounding confirmation of the power and importance of chanting the Heart Sutra for the dying.

Rosetta was the last of a flock of Rhode Island Red hens Michael, Tim, and I had raised from hatchlings for fourteen years. Rosetta had fulfilled a long and pleasant life, allowed to free-range throughout our sanctuary. She had become very affectionate and responsive to her name, and patient with all my attentions to her. She would even allow me to pick her up and set her on my knee.

A week before Easter 1999, Rosetta began to show signs of fatigue. She ate a little more slowly, and would not finish all her grain. She rested more, poking around for bugs, but with less interest in them. Over the next couple of days she would sometimes return to nearly normal. Then, just as I felt encouraged that she was all right, she would lapse back into her almost imperceptible decline. Finally, I had to admit that without question, she was preparing for The Big Leap, as it would, indeed, turn out to be.

Two days before Easter she stopped eating altogether, and I felt it was time to stop coaxing. I gave her plenty of cool, fresh water and spoke often of the journey she was about to undertake. I told her it would be wonderful, and that she would feel free. I asked her to please take messages to all kinds of folks who had gone before her, including my mother. Mostly, though, I let her just rest under her favorite rose bush. She dozed for longer periods of time, and looked quite comfortable. I'm sure she was having forays into the etheric world, testing the waters.

Late Easter evening, when all the family festivities had quieted, I went out onto the porch where I had put her in her nest for the night, and immediately sensed that she was close to dying. I scooped her up, sat on the porch floor with her cradled in my arms, and began steady breathing to quiet myself. Then I began chanting the Heart Sutra, and focused on each of the words. Simultaneously, I began the Phowa Practice, traditional in Buddhism, in which the consciousness of the dying one is transferred to the Light (or any embodiment of radiant light one believes in, such as Christ or Buddha.) In Sogyal Rinpoche's book, *The Tibetan Book of Living and Dying*, he refers to the Phowa Practice as, "The most valuable and powerful of all practices I have found in caring for the dying ...." The basic practice of Phowa is done through visualization. For Rosetta, I called upon The Christ Light to come and assist her, and I asked her to go to that Light with ease and fearlessness. I visualized her leaving her body and moving toward the Light.

As I formed these thoughts, an intense and brilliant light blazed directly in front of my closed eyes. The light was stunning, but not blinding. Instantly, I felt Rosetta's soul literally charge out of her body and rush into the light that by now surrounded us. I was overcome with the waves of joy and love emanating from the light, and I had to stop chanting and weep. Then the light was gone. I waited in the silence to see whether Rosetta's soul was still present, but there was only complete and total peace. Rosetta had died.

There are many aspects of this experience that I will never forget. The greatest gift to me, however, was the energy I felt building and deepening as I chanted the Heart Sutra, and the immediacy of the light's appearance, once I called upon it. Through this profound experience I once again learned that there is so much help available to me throughout life — and death. All I have to do is ask.

Many species of animals, including birds and insects, are sensitive to sound and tone, responding positively to chants and mantras as well as to much of the New Age music, Native American flute music, and traditional lullabies from around the world. I test any new sound or music on the general sanctuary population at Howling Success, which currently consists of dogs, cats, donkeys, goats, ducks, hens, and one extraordinary cow. Some music and sound selections put them into a state of relaxation and obvious contentment; others cause them to be more alert, yet peacefully so. Gregorian chants are appreciated by all the animals, especially during times of illness or dying.

When choosing music or sound for animals, it is best to avoid pieces that have strong rhythm or a percussion base. Keep the volume low so it won't be distracting to either the caregiver or animal. The music or sound should flow easily and lightly. Repetitive phrases, as in chants and mantras, are also good choices. Studies have shown that chants produce certain brain waves that are conducive to meditation.

Musician Robert Gass has produced a version of the Heart Sutra that has a lovely sound, easy and comfortable to sing. He has produced several tapes and CDs that have become invaluable tools in my daily work with animals. His music helps restore and maintain peace, especially among the dogs, by creating an environment that is sacred and supportive of all levels of healing. (See Resources.) This particular music is healing for those working through memories of abuse, abandonment, or loss. Some of the titles available are *Om Namaha Shivaya*, another Sanskrit chant; *Kyrie* and *Alleluia*, both chants from the Christian faith.

Gass, and his choral group, On Wings of Song, have also produced *Songs of Healing*, which has become one of my favorites, not only for myself, but for use with animals. I sing every day to those in my care and they seem to appreciate the gesture. The hens sing along! *Songs of Healing* includes titles that promote blessings, healing, and friendship, as well as support for the passage through death and beyond. One title in this collection is "Long Time Sun," a traditional song whose lyrics are:

> *May the long-time sun shine upon you,*
> *All love surround you,*
> *And the pure light within you/Guide your way home.*

Also included is the beautiful chant created by Yogananda, "Listen, Listen, Listen." The lyrics to this particular chant are repeated as follows:

> *Listen, listen, listen, to my heart's song.*
> *Listen, listen, listen to my heart's song.*
> *I will never forget you.*
> *I will never forsake you.*

These words, as with all chants, continue to build on a powerful and loving energy between the one singing and the one listening.

Some spoken tapes, mostly guided meditations used by people for healing or relaxation, seem to have a strong positive effect on animals. My favorite are the guided meditations of Stephen Levine, a meditation teacher and leader in the field of death and dying assistance. I play his *Heart Meditation* frequently, not only for animals who are dying, but for those I adopt from abandoned or abusive situations, where there is most likely a lot of fear and grief. The *Heart Meditation* is excellent for encouraging nonattachment and releasing oneself into what Levine calls "The Shared Heart," the heart of all sentient beings.

Music and sound for healing have long been considered a positive and valid means of assisting other therapies during stress, illness, or dying. There are many books and audio courses available and it is a study I highly recommend to all who work with animals.

Flower Essences

For healing and transition work I also find flower remedies, or flower essences essential. Almost daily I use flower remedies with both dying animals and as general support during illness, stress, or an overall need for well being. Flower essences are extracts drawn from the petals of various flowers, however, this method does not harm or kill the plant. The petals are then distilled in pure spring water, bottled, and preserved with apple cider vinegar or alcohol. None are toxic, even if consumed by the gallon; besides, since only drops are used at any one time, this should not be a concern. For myself, as well as with the animals, I have experienced time and again remarkable results that cannot be explained away as placebo effect.

Flower essences, akin to homeopathic medicine, provide support to the mental/emotional/physical/spiritual *whole* of an individual. They help restore a sense of balance, peace, clarity, courage and strength. I use three different sets: the Bach Flower Remedies from England found in most larger health food stores, the Perelandra Essences from Virginia, and the Anaflora Essences from California. Both the Perelandra Essences and the Anaflora Essences are available through mail order. (See Resources.)

I find flower essences both fascinating and challenging, presenting an entirely new way of healing that is unequivocally gentle, painless, noninvasive, and holistic. Dr. Edward Bach, an English physician living in the early part of the twentieth century, believed that all disease and its healing lies first in the emotional/mental fields of an individual and that all treatment should begin there. Well versed in both allopathic (so-called traditional) and homeopathic medicine, Dr. Bach was convinced that any curative or healing measures should go beyond both these methods and ought to be painless and supportive of the entire system (mental, emotional, and spiritual as well as physical) to bring all aspects of an individual back into balance and harmony. Dr. Bach spent years studying the curative essences of flowers.

Dr. Bach's thirty-eight remedies, drawing on the natural properties of certain flowers and trees combined with sunlight and the purest possible water, help alleviate such negative emotions as fear, terror, attachment, and grief that interfere with healing. Bach recognized death as a form of final healing as well. Walnut, for example, is useful in any situation of change or transition, especially dying. Gorse works magnificently for states of despair, Chicory for encouraging release. Scleranthus helps with balance and uncertainty, and Elm helps those who have a sense of being overwhelmed (good for the caregiver!).

Bach's Rescue Remedy is a combination of flower remedies no one should be without. Rescue Remedy is a combination of five of the Bach remedies: Star of Bethlehem for shock, Rock Rose for terror and panic, Impatiens for mental stress and tension, Cherry Plum for desperation, and Clematis for the indifference and disconnectedness that precedes unconsciousness. Rescue Remedy is always useful for both patient and caregiver to take simultaneously. I carry it with me wherever I go. I have used Rescue Remedy to help injured butterflies revive and go on to the next flower; helped birds in shock who have flown into glass doors and window panes; eased panic when there has been injury; and relied on Rescue Remedy for situations of shock, even when making routine trips to the veterinary hospital.

These are only a few of the Bach Remedies. A study of the entire set as well as the life and work of Dr. Bach is well worth the effort, offering information relative to everyday use for people as well as animals, wild and domesticated. Results with animals are fast and effective and in no way interfere or diminish antibiotics or other traditional medicines. Flower remedies can be given several times a day with no side effects.

When using the Bach Remedies, place four drops under or on the tongue, or on the top of the animal's head and along the base of the spine over the tail. Please don't stress yourself, or the animal by trying to pry open his mouth if the animal is unable or unwilling to open his mouth. The flower remedies help the body heal itself, rather than doing the work for the body, as allopathic drugs do. Once you notice relief, it means the body has begun the healing process, so it is important to discontinue application unless symptoms reappear. Then, and only then, is such treatment called for again.

The Perelandra Essences are formulated by Machaelle Small Wright of Jeffersonton, Virginia. At first, the study of the Perelandra Essences appears complicated, yet Wright presents material on the subject in a way that is both fascinating and easy to understand. She has several books and tapes available, all of which are well worth adding to one's library. Wright says that she draws her inspiration for creating the essences directly from nature. As with the Bach Remedies, gathering and processing of the various plants is done with respectful and appreciation for the plants, extracting the *energy* of the plant without destroying the plant itself.

There are dozens of Perelandra Essences, and in dying situations I have used broccoli, comfrey, corn, dill, salvia, summer squash, tomato, and sweet bell pepper from a group of essences that Wright calls Garden Essences. She also offers the Rose Essences (two sets) and the Nature Program Essences, many of them helpful as well. In her book, *Flower Essences*, Wright has a chapter on "Essences and the Death Process" and an in-depth section on "Flower Essences and Animals," including essential information on helping an animal through death with essences. I have found her recommendations to be most helpful and Wright is certainly a pioneer in this field.

One of the best ways to test which remedies or essences are suitable for a particular individual or situation is to use kinesiology, or simple muscle testing. A full description and instructions for kinesiology are available in both *Flower Essences* and in the pamphlet that accompanies the box of essences themselves. Essences and remedies can be used singly or in combination depending on the situation.

My three wonderful donkeys, Nori, Miso, and Julia, need to have their hooves trimmed several times a year. I have two patient, animal-caring friends who kindly volunteer their time to undertake this task. In the beginning, each session was frustrating and exhausting because the donkeys fought the whole process. We had to chase them, hold on to their lead with an iron grip, and avoid snapping teeth and kicking feet. Miso, traumatized at an early age, was especially difficult, and trimming his feet was often an impossible task.

I decided to experiment with the flower essences and put together a formula combining in one bottle filled with spring (not tap) water, several essences from both the Perelandra and Bach remedies. I added *two* drops each of the Bach Remedies and *three* drops each of the

Perelandra Essences. (The number of drops is the amount recommended by Drs. Bach and Wright.) They were as follows:

Salvia (Perelandra), for extreme stress;
Corn (Perelandra), to bring understanding and acceptance to the situation;
Aspen (Bach), for vague fears of unknown origin;
Wild Oat (Bach), for frustration and uncertainty;
Willow (Bach), for resentment over an apparently unjust situation;
Walnut (Bach), for adapting to a new situation;
Scleranthus (Bach), for balance and stability;
Impatiens (Bach), for irritability and impatience.

I also added two favorite herbs in their tincture form: Motherwort, useful for depression, and St. John's Wort, excellent for nervous situations. Then I added several teaspoons of this mixture to a handful of sliced apples that they eagerly devoured.

Granted, I was covering all bases by using so many essences. Usually, the recommendation is to limit the number of essences in any one bottle to no more than six. However, when I gave the formula to the donkeys an hour before hoof-trimming time, the change was remarkable. No more nonstop attempts to kick or haul us around the field. Now my delightful creatures stand still, all but raising their foot for an easy and painless trim. Of course, donkeys being who they are, must exhibit at least a moment of stubbornness and bray in the face of good behavior. It is, after all, part of their job description. Still, with the assistance of just a few flowers, the donkeys have become cooperative beings, even if only at foot-trimming times.

Another pioneer in the field of flower essence therapy is Sharon Callahan, based in Mt. Shasta, California. She produces the Anaflora Essences, designed for animals, as well as working as an animal communicater and consultant. Callahan's list of individual flower essences, and combination essence bottles is impressive. She will also create a bottle of essences for a specific animal's need. This is very useful for my work, since so many of the animals I care for have individual problems.

One of my favorites from her collection is "Return to Joy," a combination of essences that helps with animals who have been abandoned or abused.

Color, sound, and music are part of a vast science of healing now arising called Energy Field Work. The study and implementation of such tools will help carry all of us into a greater understanding of what healing, and indeed, what life and beyond are truly about.

TWELVE

No Such Thing as Failure

It's the day after Maxwell's death and he hovers close to me in all my thoughts, in everything I do. Rarely has a creature had such an impact on me, though his life was brief. He was my most excellent friend and the bravest mouse in all the world.

— Journal Entry, August 28, 1997

Maxwell entered my life one Thursday afternoon when my now-grown son, Michael, and his girlfriend, Jo, brought me a box full of active baby mice. They had been found in the warehouse at a local superstore after their nest had apparently been destroyed. Other workers wanted to step on the mice, squash them with boards, or run over them with pallet jacks. Jo said the women at the warehouse stood in a corner, screaming. Jo and Michael quickly scooped up the six babies and put them in a safe place with the remnants of their nest. Although fully furred out, only three of the mice had opened their eyes. They were still too young to be away from their mother, but she was not found.

"Everyone on my shift made fun of us," Michael said, "but we don't care." The three of us peered into the box and laughed as the mice ran about stiff-legged, exploring their new environment with their tails sticking straight out behind them. Every few seconds each one would stop and carefully wash his or her face and whiskers. "The people at work told us mice spread germs," Jo said, "but look how clean they are!"

Three years prior to this incident I had successfully handraised two orphaned field mice whom I had found in a sack of horse feed. So I knew how to prepare the correct formula of evaporated milk, honey, and water that had brought the field mice, Betsy and Bob, from the edge of death to full grown, self-reliant creatures. We put together a one-ounce bottle of formula with a small dropper, and put the mice in an old fish tank with a secure screen lid to keep them safe from the cats. They seemed to enjoy their new surroundings, rushing through the shredded bedding, up and over, and in and out of the smaller cardboard nesting box. They all ate well. One of the larger mice even lapped warm formula from a bottle cap. He would become Maxwell Mouse.

I wasn't sure they would survive the night, young as they were, but by morning they were all scurrying around. Only the smallest seemed more wobbly than the day before. Jo noticed some tiny mites, barely visible, on a couple of the mice. I remembered that neither Betsy nor Bob had had mites during the three weeks they lived with us, but I didn't give this situation any further thought.

That morning Jo and Michael were heading out early to North Carolina for the weekend. By the time they were packed and ready to go, it was obvious that the smallest mouse was in trouble. I reminded Michael and Jo that even if the mouse did die, it was not such a tragedy, because they had already shown great courage and compassion in rescuing the babies from the cruelty of the other workers. The little mouse would simply leave its body, I said, and go off to other realms. I promised to take the best possible care of the mice while they were gone.

By the second afternoon feeding, the mouse was running in circles, bumping into the sides of the tank and falling over. When he apparently got tired enough to stop, I placed him with the other mice huddled together under the light we had set up for heat. It was then that I discovered one of the other mice had died.

"We lost a mouse today," I told Michael that night when he called, "and I have a terrible feeling we're going to lose them all. They seem to be staggering and getting weaker, even though they're all eating well." I didn't know what the problem was and despite my brave speech that morning, I was devastated.

Hard as I tried to feed them, in the middle of the night two more died, and by Saturday morning, only two were left. The larger of the two, who seemed to be weak but holding his own, was Maxwell Mouse. It was only then, on closer examination, that the most likely cause of the problem became clear: the bedding was full of tiny mites, all engorged with blood — the blood of the baby mice. Of course! They had been infested by nearly microscopic parasites that had caused them to die from anemia. I knew this could happen to puppies and kittens infested with fleas, why not infant mice?

I asked for divine assistance Thursday evening, trying to calm my mind in order to receive some answers. Prayer has never let me down. Saturday morning with two mice each barely two inches long, staggering in front of me, I finally got some useful inspiration. With nothing to lose by this point, I decided to bathe each mouse to rid them of as many mites as possible, carefully dipping each one in a tiny tub of soapy water just up to their ears (not an easy task!) and rubbing soapy water on their heads and under their chins. They seemed to like the warm water and relaxed, allowing me to then gently dry them with the hair dryer.

The next step was as inspired as the first. Remembering that I had used Gold Bond Powder to rid myself of chiggers two years ago, I thought the boric acid in it would finish off any remaining mites. By this time I knew if I didn't try this, Maxwell and Mary would die as the others had. So once again with meticulous care, I dusted each mouse, dipping my finger in the powder, then rubbing it into their fur.

I made some oatmeal "milk" by soaking a handful of rolled oats in warm water, then adding the liquid to the original formula. To this I added Rescue Remedy. Each mouse received several drops of this mixture and Maxwell began to respond. I was delighted. Sadly, Mary Mouse died in the afternoon, just too weak to recover her strength.

Maxwell was now the one survivor. He wobbled over and placed one tiny paw, then his head, across Mary's body. I removed her body, replacing it with an old stuffed animal that I thought might help comfort him. The small pink and fuzzy toy pig was flat in shape and under the lamp, quite warm. I laid the pig on its back and sure enough, Maxwell climbed up across the stuffed toy's body to lay his paw, and then his head, across the snout. There he closed his eyes and slept.

The oatmeal formula seemed to give him the strength I had hoped for, and the mites were all but gone. That evening he scurried over to the bottle cap and for the first time since Friday morning, lapped at the milk. He would take a few steps away, then, as if to say, "Hmmm, pretty good. I think I'll have some more," he'd turn around and hurry back for a few more laps. Then he was off exploring again.

Maxwell was a tidy mouse, careful to balance on his long back legs and with attention to every detail, wash hands, face, whiskers, and stomach. So carefully would he first wash the inside of his hands to wet them, then rub them down across his nose and over his whiskers, a procedure he repeated for as much as a minute at a time. Then he would scamper up, hand over foot, across his pig to wrap himself around the warm snout, or lie contentedly under one of the soft ears. I enjoyed hand feeding him, holding him so tenderly between the palm of my hand and forefinger, his tiny head poking out over my thumb. Each time I offered the end of the eye dropper, he would take hold of it with both front paws and suck the formula. Once again he could move around the area without staggering, his tail straight out behind him. Maxwell was doing so well I promised him I would import a small white mouse for him if he would just survive.

But by the 2 AM feeding, Maxwell began his long descent once again, not quite as strong as earlier in the evening, not drinking quite as much formula, lapping only once from the bottle cap with my encouragement. He lost his balance several times while bathing himself and he leaned against his pig, rather than climb up to the snout. Stubbornly, I refused to give up and encouraged him to keep up the fight for life. I wasn't seeing any more mites on him or the bedding, so what could be the problem?

Sunday morning, 9 o'clock feeding, I knew I was losing Maxwell. My despair was overwhelming. I went into the garden and picked a brilliant yellow chrysanthemum blossom and brought it upstairs. "A get well present," I said, as I laid the flower next to him. "Just in case you might consider staying here." He raised his tiny nose, whiskers vibrating, and sniffed at the fragrance. I still hoped ....

Just before one in the afternoon, I made fresh oatmeal and added more Rescue Remedy. It had worked so well before, maybe .... But when I got upstairs, his frail body lay on its side in the middle of the tank. He was dying. Even so, when I called his name, he twitched his nose and whiskers and tried to raise his head.

Suddenly, I knew I had to take Maxwell outside. As I reached for him it was almost as if someone else was guiding my hand. I realized this mouse (as well as his brothers and sisters), born in a warehouse, then rushed to a glass tank inside a house, had never seen the beautiful natural Earth. Unlike Betsy and Bob, Maxwell would never have the chance to run freely through the fields and nibble on seeds, or feel the sun on his coat.

It was a brilliant sunny afternoon. I carried Maxwell around the flower gardens, propped up between my palm and thumb. I let his head poke out so he could see, hear, smell, and feel with his whiskers, all the delights around us. "Here, Maxwell, these are hollyhocks. And look, over here are asters, and these are morning glories ...." Gently, I touched his feet to the soft soil, then the grass, holding him upright as he was no longer strong enough to stand alone. "I want you to know and remember all of this, Maxwell, so when you come back, you'll know where to come to!" He wiggled his whiskers with all the energy he could gather, his bright, tiny black eyes watching me. I felt I was in the presence of a great being, a soul without bounds, about to be released. "Listen, those sounds are birds singing," I said, "and the waterfall in the garden pond, and the crickets, they're singing for you." We rested together in silence.

"Now Maxwell," I said, getting down to business, "there are some friends I want you to say hi to for me when you get to the other side, okay?" His nose twitched weakly; I knew he understood me. "There are all your brothers and sisters; I'm sure they're right here waiting for you. And your mother, if she's around, too. And please, will you look up my grandmother? I've asked her to help you cross over. She's great, you'll really like her."

I just kept talking. He kept listening and watching me closely. "You've been a terrific mouse, Maxwell," I said, "a miracle in your own right." Then, knowing his death was imminent, I began to help him prepare for the transition. He was showing physical signs of dying, the jerking of his legs, the gasping for air. Unfortunately, he was struggling against the process.

"Please let go of your body now, don't be afraid," I said quietly. "I'll be okay. But will you come back to me?" He was nearly gone now and I had forgotten to make this vital request. I hoped he had heard me, because then he was gone. One simple exhale and his body settled quietly, softly into my hand. Suddenly, I felt his presence in the air, the sky, the bird song, and the waterfall. I cried, of course.

That evening when Michael and Jo returned from their trip, we held a ceremony, burying the mice in the garden among the flowers. We talked about all that had happened. There was the derision of their fellow workers who thought Michael and Jo were strange. Then the incident itself of finding the babies and their brief and seemingly tragic demise here. What did it all mean? We found no immediate answers.

But as the hours passed, and then the days, I was aware that Maxwell's energy surrounded me. Neither pest nor varmint, as mice are commonly considered, Maxwell clearly demonstrated his gentle, curious personality and soul. As with all the other creatures I have known, he proved that all beings are precious, each one worthy of respect, love, and every effort to support them in life and through the process of death. Likewise, his miracle shines through the unwavering courage of two young people and their determination to speak firmly about, and act upon, what they believe, even in the face of ridicule from peers.

Even after all my years of working with animals, the question, "Did I somehow fail?" sometimes lurks on the edge of my mind. Animals are subject to all kinds of accidents, diseases, neglect and abuse, all of which tip their scales too heavily on the side of Things-Going-Wrong. In addition, animals rarely complain, so it can be difficult to detect physical ailments. From an unhealthy gum situation to cancer, or lupus, or even diabetes, sometimes it can take awhile before I realize there is a serious problem.

For example, a kitten appeared on the front stone step to the garden late one afternoon, looking like a miniaturized version of our cat, Lucy. The gray-and-white kitten just sat there, front feet placed carefully together, the size of a six-week old, no more.

Instantly, we welcomed him into the family and named him Luke. We gave him the best food and toys (being a kitten he needed a good supply). At the animal hospital, Dr. Partridge gave Luke all the necessary tests and vaccinations, and estimated that he was not six weeks old, but six *months* old, stunted through malnutrition, probably from abandonment.

Luke seemed so sad and quiet, and most likely still in shock from simply trying to survive on his own. Perhaps he was trying to understand what he had done to cause his previous family to abandon him.

Animal communicators will often receive such a message from an animal who has been abused or abandoned. I have found this to be an important consideration in working with animals who are chronically ill or lethargic.

Three months went by and although Luke ate well and grew into a lanky teenager, he moved as if he were a hundred years old, his face solemn and sad, his eyes deep in his head. He refused all our attempts to make him play. He never chased leaves or butterflies, balls of aluminum foil, or braids of string. Luke ate ravenously and slept and slept and slept. When he moved, it was as if every step was agony and his feet were dragging lead.

Luke's too-thin frame concerned me, as well as his dull, greasy coat, but Dr. Partridge, knowing the stages of young cathood better than I, assured me he was probably full of parasites, and a good worming would straighten things out. So we proceeded in that direction. At the end of the treatment, Luke was even thinner, quieter, and obviously in greater distress. When he had been living with us for six months with no improvement, it was time for a full blood profile to see exactly what was going on.

The results were stunning. "If you had told me this cat was diabetic," Dr. Partridge said, "I would have told you the chances were nearly nonexistent." Not only that, Luke was diagnosed as a juvenile diabetic, the most serious kind, meaning his body made no insulin of its own at all. How he ever survived his first year of life in such a condition is a mystery to everyone.

Of course, I was full of guilt. How could I have allowed this beautiful creature to be in such distress all these months?. I mourned the loss of his kittenhood, all those days of adventure, troublemaking, curiosity, and rampant energy. I felt I was to blame for not taking more notice or action much sooner. Failure was a concept I clung to, despite my family and friends kindly telling me otherwise.

Eventually, I allowed myself the idea that perhaps I had really done the best I could. I had followed the most logical course of action, and of greatest importance, the end result was success, considering that diabetes is a workable condition and I was prepared to help Luke live out his life in the best possible manner. Rather than continue to berate myself, considering that Luke understood my distressed thoughts, I decided that the most helpful attitude to hold was that from that point on, we would work together towards healing.

Five years later, with twice-daily insulin injections and carefully monitored meals to regulate his blood sugar levels, Luke is a strong nine-and-a-half pound cat with a glossy, smooth coat and radiant green eyes. A white spiral that twists up around his nose to his forehead gives him the appearance of a mystical creature merely inhabiting a cat's body. His name, alone, is significant. When he first appeared, I wanted desperately to give him a sweet, soft kitten name, something like Beau or Whiskers. However, the name Luke was insistent, and in the end, I surrendered to the name. It wouldn't surprise me if he had chosen the name of the great physician, St. Luke. Aren't cats capable of anything?

I learned about failure from a little gray mouse and a little gray cat. They each taught me that no matter how much I think I know, it is never enough to solve all the problems or answer all the questions, all the time. Now I would redefine that terrible state of mind called "Sense of Failure" to read: "Being Human," — the state of *not perfect and it's okay; just trying to do the best I can with all my heart.*

THIRTEEN

Animals and Grieving

There is another facet to grief that is often neglected when an animal dies: the grieving by other animals in the family. Time and again I have seen animals feel loss when another leaves, the pain sometimes so intense that it results in a serious illness, or even their own death.

I will testify from experience that all manner of animals regard death — both their own and that of others around them — with more than just fascination or fear. When Corky, my beloved canine friend of fifteen years died the day after her birthday in April 1995, I brought her body home from the animal hospital. I wrapped it carefully in white cloth, and laid it on the front porch. The other dogs knew she was gone and would not cross the place where her bed had been, even though it was in a major traffic area between the kitchen and front porch. I had already removed the bed and washed it. It had been the same situation following Waggy's death. After she died, not one dog would climb into the chair she had rested in that final year. Finally, I took the chair from the living room.

With Corky's passing, the hour before her last trip to the hospital had been violent and confusing. She had a sudden grand mal seizure and the other dogs were frightened by it. When Doug and I returned later that night after having her put to sleep, the remaining members of the dog family were exceptionally quiet, too quiet. I could have used some noise and distraction!

The following day I dug the hole for Corky's body in a beautiful bed of violets. I was about to lay her body in the grave when I looked up, sensing a strong presence nearby. There was Sam, always my guardian and the alpha dog, watching intently. As I had done for Stef with Little Eddie's body, I let Sam see Corky's body, explained as best I could what I was about to do, and then folded the sheet back over our friend. Sam seemed to understand, telling me so by looking straight into my eyes and then bowing his head — Sam's way of communicating with me. Together, we buried Corky and honored our very special friend.

Steffie chose to leave a healthy young body to be with Little Eddie, understanding that he was no longer alive once we presented his body to her. I believe it was at that moment that she made her decision to die. I was impressed by Thomas the cat's reaction to Penny Reynolds's death. He had stayed close by us throughout her dying. At the time I thought it amazing that one animal would care so much about another, giving her support throughout her dying. I was especially impressed that a cat would care that much about a dog.

Thomas was remarkable in many ways and had shown a strong attachment to other animals before Penny. His best buddy, Benjamin, another black-and-white stray cat we had adopted, was killed by a car. When his body was laid on our neighbor's lawn by some thoughtful person, Thomas lay down right next to Benjamin, his front leg draped across the cold body. When our neighbor found them, Thomas was so quiet she thought he was dead as well. We had to lift Thomas off of Benjamin, explaining as best we could that his friend would not be coming home. Thomas moped for weeks after the incident before apparently resigning himself to life as an only cat. Naturally, in our house this would never be a permanent situation, and within a month we had taken in another stray feline in need of a family.

Thomas was, in fact, the first animal to show me that humans are not the only ones to mourn the loss of a friend. Animals feel the void left in the wake of death. Therefore, it is vital to take such grieving creatures right on through the resolution process. This means that as a caregiver, I am always acutely observant of any signs of grief in the other animals, such as despondency, loss of appetite, sudden aggressive behavior, sudden loss of weight, a desire to remain in dark corners, refusal to socialize with other animals or people. They may develop a dull coat, or severe allergies, or begin to lose eyesight or hearing. If all disease is preceded by a breakdown in the mental/emotional bodies as so many doctors and psychologists in the field of mind/body medicine now know to be true, then it is not such an outrageous proposition that in animals physical decline would follow intense grief.

Resolution in such cases asks great patience on the caregiver's part because any explanation regarding death will naturally involve abstract principles and animals best understand humans when clear, precise mental images are offered to them. But I never hesitate to speak with the other animals in my family in a direct and honest manner, forming the clearest images I can. The conversation is always one-sided: I talk, my animal friend watches me patiently, sometimes grooms him or herself, or takes a brief nap. But I never fool myself; they do understand and they very much appreciate my concern for their feelings.

So when I speak with them, I trust that the creature in question will understand the images I form as thought, and sense the color and tone reflected by my words. I remind my friend that the one who has died did so in his or her own time and is delighted to be just where he or she is. I reassure them that they can experience the soul aspect of their departed companion. I know Thomas was aware of Penny leaving her body.

But sometimes, despite my efforts, the grieving will carry animals out of life. The situation with Sally illustrates this well. I found Sally standing on our sidewalk one morning in April 1980 looking poignantly at our back door. A spunky black-and-white, full-coated border collie, she was bright-eyed and determined to be friends. Obviously, she felt right at home with us. Within twenty-four hours I had located the neighbors with whom she lived, but they were eager for me to adopt her. She was pregnant and they had planned to shoot her. Sally, as I subsequently named her, certainly had an excellent sense of timing and direction, if not foresight.

Sally moved right in, as they all tend to do, soon to become a staunch and much-loved member of the ranks. She became best pals with Parsley who, also a reject from the same neighbors, had "adopted" us two years earlier. Parsley and Sally were a couple of charmers and they became inseparable.

Sally had six pups under the house three weeks later and was an excellent mother for the full six weeks before weaning. During that time she rarely left home and Parsley stayed close to her. Four of the pups were adopted and we kept two, Waggy and Corky. After that, Sally and Parsley began disappearing into the mountains, sometimes to my great frustration and concern, for two or three days at a time. Invariably, they would resurface in good condition and spirits, despite being covered in burrs, ticks, and red mud. They ate together, slept together, played together, and had become one indivisible unit.

On an early December morning two years later, they set off for their tour of the mountains and as usual, did not return for dinner that evening. It was the beginning of hunting season and I was uneasy. At dawn the next morning Sally returned alone, dragging herself up the drive and into the house. Immediately, I sensed something was wrong and indeed it became apparent as the days passed that Parsley would not be following her home.

As my weekly trips to the animal shelter continued over the year in a heartbreaking search for my lost friend, I encountered many wonderful homeless beagles who, I was told, had most likely been stolen during hunting season from late November to early January, used for hunting, then abandoned. This was the most probable fate that had befallen Parsley.

Whatever did happen out there in those mountains was undoubtedly witnessed by Sally and it permanently traumatized her. She became increasingly frightened of loud noises. And raised, argumentative voices sent her into uncontrolled shivering. Her refusal to even step outside the door without me right beside her was a tremendous reversal of her previous urge to roam. She never did return to the mountains.

The fears Sally developed took a swift and vicious toll on her body. She became increasingly allergic to everything. Dr. Partridge said she had a flea allergy, but for all the baths and dips I had given her, and the recommended medication, her condition did not improve. In the process Sally had scratched herself so raw that she had barely any hair left on her body by the time she died. I had resorted to buying and dressing her in children's T-shirts to protect her delicate skin.

Subtle things could send her into a frenzy of scratching: The sound of the vacuum cleaner, the kids setting off fireworks; guns fired even at great distances, and at one point my coughing bouts due to a life-threatening case of bronchitis. There were times when she would watch me closely, and if I started to cough, she would sit up, scratch, and cough as well until I stopped.

Sally dropped weight, and developed chronic eye and ear infections that could not be cured. Generally, Sally seemed to be retreating from life. Finally, after much struggle she died of congestive heart failure, or it would seem, from a broken heart.

⌒

Brewster Rooster, a resident bird at the sanctuary some years back, reinforced my lessons on animal grieving. In addition, he confirmed my personal opinions on the great loving capacity and intelligence of chickens.

Following the habits of roosters in general, Brewster took up with one particularly stunning hen named Ms. Peach. But unlike other roosters, he did not run from hen to hen, nor trade in hen friends in a day or two. Loyalty was his lot, and in his eyes (or so it sure seemed to us) Ms. Peach was his love for life. They slept side by side in the barn at night high above the snoozing goats. They enjoyed their days roaming gardens and fields together, with Brewster searching out the most delectable insects for her.

Six months into their relationship, Ms. Peach suddenly became ill, and despite all efforts to save her, declined rapidly. Quite softly and without struggle or complaint, she sighed twice and eased from life.

Brewster watched from the field, his head tilted to one side. That night he slept alone on their perch, leaving her spot vacant. By the next morning he began to refuse food, even to move far from the field where they had usually spent their days together. By the third day of such obvious depression, Brewster sat hunched in the tall grass, his magnificent head touching the ground. And there he, too, passed from life, still mourning the loss of his beloved best friend. I believe Ms. Peach was waiting for him. Some skeptics might argue that both Sally's and Brewster's deaths were due to illness. When Brewster Rooster lost his companion, his decline was obvious and steady, despite all encouraging words and efforts on my part. While at first I feared some deadly virus was moving through the flock, no one else of the twenty-five remaining hens showed any signs of illness and no others died during that entire year.

Many companionships have formed among our animals, especially among the dogs, the donkeys, and the goats. Both donkeys and goats form strong family bonds that last for life and any separation of the family is extremely difficult for them. In the summer of 1995 when thirteen-year old Phoebe the goat died, I was very concerned about the four remaining members of the herd, who were also very old. Emily and Isabelle were both fourteen, and Shanti and Amanda were thirteen. For weeks after Phoebe's death the goats refused to leave their pen to graze or roam the woods. Their coats, usually shiny and full, began to look dull and thin. Acting on intuition, I adopted a six-month old wether whom we named Patrick, for good luck. My hunch worked.

Immediately, the girls perked up, joined forces, and instead of mothering the little guy as I had hoped, took to systematically beat him up. They didn't hurt Patrick, they just wanted to keep him in his place. Within two weeks Patrick had gained their respect and he became a beloved member of the herd. Within three weeks of Patrick's arrival, the girls were out grazing once again and their coats had returned to full health.

Beyond all rational thought on my part, I now know that an animal's grieving can be so profound that nothing will stop his or her choice to literally run from life. My beloved duck Steffie decided to leave after Little Eddie's death and even though I missed her, I was glad she was reunited with her life partner. Her departure seemed so natural and easy; however, a dog named CeeCee, taught me a very different lesson. She was my reminder that just when I think I know it all, it's time for the bottom to fall out of my life and a serious adjustment to occur in my learning about life and death.

With all my years of experience with elderly and special-needs animals, I felt comfortable with the arrival of CeeCee to my sanctuary in May 1998. There was considerable synchronicity of events around this new dog, too obvious to ignore, intriguing enough to catch my curiosity.

My little hound-mix, Emmett, had died suddenly and unexpectedly due to a previously undiagnosed malignant tumor on his aorta that had ruptured. With no forewarning, I was unable to adequately prepare myself, or Emmett, for his passage. I accepted the process as timely to Emmett's own evolution, and I knew there was nothing that could have been done medically to save him. Still, I was drained by the inevitable grief. In addition, my mother's illness and subsequent death four months earlier had taken about everything out of me. I clearly remember not asking, but *telling* the universe to *not send any more creatures at this time!* A reasonable request, I thought: I needed rest and less to do, not more.

But *two* days after Emmett's departure, the phone rang and a young woman named Beth began talking to me, sounding desperate. Her mother, Mary, had died nine months earlier, she said, leaving Beth and her brother without a home and with several dogs and one cat. All the animals were being taken care of, except one — a fifteen-year-old collie-yorkie mix, CeeCee, who was partially deaf, senile, and had some cataracts. She also had a mid-level heart murmur, enough to slow her down and be of concern, but not exceptionally serious, yet. Of course, when Beth and her brother tried to find CeeCee a safe home, nobody wanted her. Clearly, she was at the end of her life and would require extra care and daily medication. Such animals rarely have a chance at a new home.

CeeCee had been her mother's favorite dog, Beth said, and before her mother became ill, Mary had worried about losing CeeCee to old age. Neither Beth nor her brother could bear to put CeeCee to sleep, but would have to if no home was found. Beth's new apartment was too small, and her kind landlady was already bending the rules by letting Beth keep her mother's smaller dogs. I promised to put the word out and see if I could help, but after a week of intense searching, I still had come up with nothing. Time had run out for CeeCee and Beth. It was a miserable situation at best.

After reasonable consideration (and much urging by my inner self) I agreed to adopt CeeCee. Obviously, she should be here, I thought. It was as if Emmett had left in order to make room for her. With fifteen other dogs, I could not have even considered a new dog if Emmett hadn't died. In addition, I felt an instant rapport with both Beth and her brother. We had long healing conversations about losing our mothers. CeeCee certainly seemed to be a healer and messenger for all three of us.

From the first, CeeCee was a very sweet, gentle, and polite dog. A joy to be with, yet, something was wrong. She immediately began to behave in a way I had not seen before. Daily, she paced the house or along the fence in the dogs' garden, as if looking for a way out. It was as if she were searching for someone. Mary, perhaps? Apparently, she had been as devoted to her previous person, as Mary had been to her. At night, in order for CeeCee to rest, I had to sleep next to her, continually reassuring her that she was safe. Otherwise, she would pace and bark, pace and bark. The nights with CeeCee got to be very long!

On the hunch that she was looking and calling for Mary, I had several long talks with CeeCee, trying to explain about Mary's death, that Mary was fine, and she would see CeeCee again. I promised her the best of care and my loyalty and love to the end and told her how much I enjoyed her company. I hoped CeeCee would choose to stay with us a while longer, despite her advanced age.

But CeeCee, being her own intelligent self, had other ideas. On a Monday morning, two weeks after she came to live with me, she escaped. It was one of those rare, odd events that scream of "Meant-To-Be." Unfortunately, being human and short-sighted, I suffered greatly with guilt.

I had opened the sliding glass doors to the front porch to let in some fresh air on this warm day, being careful to firmly close the screen while I was cleaning. An hour later, heading down to the basement to do laundry, I neglected to close the glass door, as had always been my practice. This time, I completely forgot, leaving no more than a two-foot width of screen door exposed. Then I went downstairs.

When I came up five minutes later, I immediately sensed something was wrong, and it concerned CeeCee. The screen had been pushed back just enough, and CeeCee was no where in sight. The most peculiar part was that not one of the other dogs tried to leave, even though the smaller ones certainly could have easily gotten through the opening. Furthermore, CeeCee had managed to then squeeze through the porch gate railings, which would have seemed impossible because of her size.

Though we all searched until after dark, I knew CeeCee was gone. Between her inability to hear us call, her confusion due to senility, and miles of mountain land in all directions, the chances of finding her were minimal. Early the next morning we posted notices everywhere, and a caring neighbor called to say CeeCee was lying on her front lawn, dead.

I was devastated. I felt cheated, not being there for her dying. And, there was incredible guilt for being careless with the door. But most of all, I felt as if I had let down Beth and her brother when they had entrusted their mother's dog to me. I doubted myself.

After two days of despair, I felt compelled to take up pencil and paper and if nothing else, access my inner self. Perhaps I would reach CeeCee, wherever she was. The words flowed easily through my mind to paper, reassuring me. CeeCee thanked me for my love and care during her brief stay with me. She wanted me to know that she was very happy to be reunited with Mary, for whom she had mourned and searched ever since Mary's death. Speaking with Beth three months later, I learned that it was only after her mother's death that CeeCee began pacing and barking, escaping several times while still at Mary's old house before it was sold.

CeeCee's message made sense and I believe it really did come from the spirit/soul of that sweet dog. CeeCee's grief, so deep and unable to be resolved in this life, could only find relief by literally running to her favorite person. A weak heart was the perfect avenue of escape. That grief overrode all other words or comfort I had given her, and although she regretted causing me pain, she did what she had to do. Could I have done anything to stop her? In retrospect, I doubt it. If not then, she would have found another way out, later. For awhile I was angry with CeeCee, and one day I sat on the bench by her garden and told her everything I felt. *How could you do this to me?* I asked. *Didn't you know how much I hurt? Couldn't it have happened another way?* Then I was gently reminded, in my mind, of all those times I couldn't and wouldn't have let her go. I then realized and accepted that CeeCee acted in the best way she knew.

Perhaps I will meet CeeCee again and get to know her much better. And if I am fortunate, I will meet Mary as well. CeeCee offered a powerful lesson on listening, and allowing, and accepting the power of grief. For CeeCee, it was a dog grieving the death of her human companion.

FOURTEEN

The Other Side of the Bridge

When an animal approaches that bridge of transition called death, I remind myself that my friend is simply coming to a juncture between worlds. She is not disappearing into nothing. And I trust that the beings of light are also present to help ease her over. My job is to visualize that expansive bridge and the spirit guides.

When I am able to be fully mindful of such a process, sensations of grief, anger, and loss simply evaporate, at least temporarily, so that I can help make my companion's passage out of body as easy and comfortable as possible. When the transition is complete, and she has separated from her body, all I need to do is return my focus to the beings of light. Miraculously, the grief momentarily lessens; I know they are here for me, too.

Yet, when the death of an animal is complete, I often feel suddenly and desperately alone. The silence and stillness of the lifeless body, the finality of death, can be overwhelming. Eventually, I emerge from the whirlwind of such an intense time. Relieved that the animal's soul is free of pain and suffering, now I can begin to mend my own pain of loss through the ceremonies of grieving, burial of the body, and establishing a memorial.

But one sweet cat named Patches taught me, through her passage, that even though an animal has died, I, as caregiver, still have work to do. The focus of the work is on behalf of that animal's soul. Where is that soul once death is complete? And, how is that soul adjusting to her new surroundings? Patches showed me that immediately following death, the animal's soul may still be very close. And, that soul may need my help to adjust to her new state of being.

I called Patches my Halloween cat. She was a thin tortoise shell with high, puffed-out cheeks, and wide yellow eyes. At fourteen, she loped rather than walked across the floor and she had the loudest, most persistent purr of any cat I have ever known.

Patches and her sister, Snowball, came to live with us when they were thirteen. Both adjusted well despite the unexpected and traumatic changes of entering our busy sanctuary at such an advanced age. Shortly after joining our family, Patches developed a hyperthyroid condition that required careful monitoring and daily medication. Once again she took the situation in stride, always eager to greet us as her best friends, purring and meowing her contentment.

Early in 1999, Patches began to lose ground with her weight and her breathing. She had difficulty eating despite an excellent appetite and increasingly became too wobbly to do her famous lope across the floor. Michael and I took her to the animal hospital, and returned home to await the diagnosis. When Dr. Helle Stewart, an associate of Dr. Partridge, called, her news was sad. Patches had developed a condition causing air to be gathering outside her lungs. Because of this, Patches had partial collapse of both lungs and increasing overall distress. She could no longer eat and breathe comfortably at the same time, and every movement was painful. At her age, there was no successful treatment available.

Dr. Stewart suggested that we consider having Patches released from her pain. Michael and I agreed with her recommendation for euthanasia, but we wanted to be there. I needed to let Patches know what was going to happen. Dr. Stewart kindly agreed to keep Patches on oxygen until we arrived.

"Patches is a wonderful cat," Dr. Stewart said when we entered the exam room. "But she doesn't like us working on her. She will probably struggle when we give her the shot, and it could get rough." She started to lift Patches to take her into another room.

"No," I replied firmly, "we want to be with her, that's why we're here." Then even I was surprised when I heard myself say, "I'll talk to her, let her know exactly what's going to happen. It will probably make a difference in how she reacts. It always does." I had never told this to a veterinarian before, even though I knew it was true. I had always been too shy. Dr. Stewart hardly knew me, but to her credit she only nodded, and offered to let us have a few minutes alone with Patches.

When she left the room, Michael and I talked to Patches. By now Patches was so weak she needed to be supported while she gasped for breath. We stroked her and gently assured her that soon all her pain would be gone. I told her that Dr. Stewart would give her an injection to help ease her out of her body. "You won't need that old, frail body where you are going to, Patches," I told her. "You are going to a wonderful place where you will be so happy!" She wasn't tense, but didn't seem to be listening either. I continued talking to her. I knew she heard me on some level of her being. "You need to help Dr. Stewart," I said, "by being very calm and just letting go. Michael and I will be here to help you, and you know we will always love you."

Dr. Stewart reentered the room with a veterinary technician. They stood on either side of Patches while I sat at the head of the exam table, cradling her head in my hands. I spoke quietly to Patches, continually telling her that everything was okay, that she could relax and begin letting go of her body. Just as Dr. Stewart was ready to insert the needle into Patches' hind leg, once again I surprised myself by saying aloud, "Okay, Patches, this is the part where you help Dr. Stewart." If there were any lifted eyebrows, I didn't see them.

Patches neither whimpered nor flinched as Dr. Stewart gave her the shot. I watched Patches' eyes as she changed her focus from me to within herself until the pupils became fixed and her head eased over in my hands. Her soul was gone. While her heart continued to beat for a few seconds, again I spoke aloud to her, encouraging her to let go.

Dr. Stewart sighed with relief. "I love it when it's easy like that," she said.

"It always is, when you let them know what is happening each step of the way," I said. "Dying is much less frightening."

Michael was called from the room and Dr. Stewart said quietly, "I'll just give you some time to be with Patches," a gesture I truly appreciated. Now I was alone with the small, lifeless body of my Halloween cat.

I closed my eyes and visualized on her sweet face. Suddenly, I saw her in my mind: She looked luminous and healthy. She appeared to be sitting up on her haunches and looking up and around her as she moved her head back and forth repeatedly. I received the strong impression that she was confused, wondering, *Where am I? What's happened? How did I get here?* She seemed disoriented by her new surroundings, although she was not frightened. I again focused all my thought toward her, saying, "You're perfectly safe, Patches. You're in that wonderful place I told you about. Notice how easily you can breathe now."

I couldn't seem to get her attention, although I felt as if my words were reaching her. She continued to turn her head back and forth, looking everywhere, but her expression began to shift from one of confusion to one of absolute wonderment and joy. She glowed!

"Patches," I said, sending my thought as strongly as I could, "look around you. There has to be a being of light there. Go with that being, follow that light — the light is there to guide you on." Again I felt as if she had received my message even though she did not seem to be aware of me. I had the comfortable sensation that from now on that the soul that was Patches, was going to be fine.

At that precise moment, the vet technician entered the room, and I opened my eyes.

The process of death and the efforts of a caregiver transcend all religions and philosophies. The Buddhists, in particular, work with a person to help him or her prepare for death and leave the body. Buddhists continue to assist that soul for days and sometimes weeks following death, through the next stages that soul will experience. An excellent, detailed explanation of this practice can be found in *The Tibetan Book of Living and Dying* by Sogyal Rinpoche. I had read of this practice before knowing Patches but had never applied it. My experience with her confirmed for me the importance of continuing my support of the soul until I sense that the animal's soul feels safe and at peace.

Patches's heart stopped within seconds of being given the injection, typical with euthanasia, causing her to experience confusion by so sudden a jolt out of her body. If she had experienced a natural, slower dying, I believe her soul would probably have spent considerable time moving between earth and the etheric, preparing for the transformation. When the final crossover did occur, the etheric plane would, by then, be at least somewhat familiar and the transition less of a shock. This seemed to be my mother's experience during her passage. After ten intense days of obviously moving in and out of her body at precise intervals, my mother's soul seemed to finally, simply ease away.

Because of Patches I now ask for time alone with the animal once euthanasia is complete. I continue to send reassuring thoughts to help that animal's soul safely on his or her journey. Hopefully, every veterinary hospital will eventually have a room set aside specifically for times when an animal must be euthanized. Such a room would provide a quiet, less austere atmosphere, with a tape or CD player available for playing supportive music or chanting. Such a room would also have a comfortable chair to allow a people to be more relaxed with their animal companions prior to, and after, euthanasia. I believe that someday veterinarians will understand the importance of hospice support for animals and their humans — before, during, and after that animal's death.

⌣

After an animal friend has died, and I feel confident that her soul is comfortable with her new existence on the etheric plane, I tend to myself for awhile. Experiencing the death of another is difficult, no doubt about it. Anyone who would say, "Come on now, it was only an animal," or "Don't you think he's better off?" or "So when are you going to get another one?" truly diminishes the power of a relationship with an animal. Yes, I am relieved my friend is no longer suffering or struggling, and I miss him. I can feel both of those things at the same time.

When anyone asks me if I plan to immediately adopt another animal to soothe my grief, I can only tell them that nothing and no one could possibly replace that unique creature who has just died. Not even the cutest pup or kitten could adequately fill the void in which I find myself, nor should another animal be made to. When another creature in need finds his or her way to my door, then I will welcome that one and begin a new relationship with all the enthusiasm that I had for my previous companion. It's all part of loving another — loving someone so much that their essential "soul" nature becomes entwined with mine. This is the concept of communion, or interconnectedness. Each one, a reflection of myself and of the whole of life, brings her or his gift of uniqueness that cannot be replaced by another.

So, when someone I love dies, a part of me dies as well. It's part of the process. I accept that and move forward, but that is not to say I don't feel pain and grieve. Two months from now I may find myself bursting into tears without warning, or even five years later staring into space as I think about that beloved one. I still think about Tevy, a wonderful old duck, three years after her death. During her last winter, she slept on the porch at night in a protected cage. I still look up in the sky at dawn and find our wishing star, the one I always pointed out to Tevy as I carried her each morning out to the duck house to join the rest of the flock. "Tevy," I still whisper to her, even though she is long gone, "Look, how bright our star is! I wish for you a remarkable journey and a return someday to this sanctuary." The emptiness that follows the death of another never quite disappears and like the soft spot on the top of a newborn's head, remains a vulnerable part of anyone who loves another.

But even so, when love is freely given to another, love is always returned. It's one of those inexplicable universal laws that finds definition best in the application. Repeatedly I have experienced that the more I give, the more I receive. Thus, the more I give, the more I have in my heart to give. As long as I am willing to accept such a law then there is always room for another companion, someone with whom to share all that love. That does not mean I replace the ones who have gone on, nor erase their memory, but to enrich and expand upon what those particular animals gave to me.

My beloved Sadie had been with me for over seventeen years and we had been inseparable the entire time. Because of our closeness, her death was difficult for me and I was especially drained emotionally and physically from other family problems. But the Great Mystery sent not one, but *two* new dogs into my life barely four weeks after Sadie's departure. Both creatures were in desperate need of major surgery, love, attention, and nutritious food. I will admit that often I have wondered if Sadie didn't direct them to our door to help ease me through my grief. I wouldn't put it past her.

If the creature who has just died in my care is a casual acquaintance, for example, an insect or wildling, then wishing them a happy and blessed journey is usually sufficient resolution for me. However, long-time companions, such as Sadie and Waggy, require more intense resolution on my part. For anyone in such a situation, I offer the following:

LET GO OF GUILT

Guilt is one of the most difficult emotions from which to disentangle. I learned through my experience with Waggy to go day by day. And during our last week together, I went hour by hour, evaluating what I thought she needed, and when. I had to rely on Waggy to tell me when it was time to help her on, and she did. Because I made myself pay attention to her signals, rather than simply fretting about her condition, the whole process of decision, follow-through, and assistance through her dying flowed quite smoothly. I emerged from the other side of such a traumatic time, completely without guilt. What a relief!

The only other time I can honestly say I had no regrets, no guilt over the decision to euthanize one of the animals, was many years ago when my cat, Noah, developed leukemia. The disease had just been discovered in cats and all I understood was that he was suddenly very sick. Dr. Partridge advised me that even though Noah was barely two years old, he had no chance of recovering. Still, I was, as always, very cautious about rushing to end his life.

Doug and I have two special friends, Jane and Steve, who are both gifted with the ability of clairvoyance. They use their gift to help others and their "readings" have always proved to be spiritual as well as accurate. When the veterinarian gave me the prognosis for Noah, I immediately phoned Jane and asked if she would try and contact Noah by way of telepathy for his input on the situation. Was it his time to go? If so, did he want us to help him on? Was he in pain, or suffering in any way? Today, animal communicators are readily available to do such telepathic work, but back then it was unheard of, and quite an unusual request. But I trusted Jane's ability completely.

To confirm accuracy, her husband, Steve, went into another room and asked the identical set of questions at the same time as Jane. When I phoned back, their separate answers matched perfectly:

Yes, Noah told Jane and Steve, he did have leukemia, but no, he was not in any pain. He had completed everything he had come into this life to do, and now he was choosing to leave. He would be pleased if we helped him move on because he really had no need to linger here on Earth.

I knew with absolute certainty that the message was valid and I agreed to have Noah euthanized. I have never regretted that decision.

Since that experience I have called on the expertise of an animal communicator when I was uncertain as to the correct course to take.

But if after receiving their communication I feel at all unsure, I wait until I have inner confidence that it is time to assist the death process. Again, by speaking directly with the creature and asking for her signal as to what *she* wants, I find that any decision carries far less guilt on my part.

Still I ask myself, "Could I have done more?" "Should I have done this instead of that?" "Why didn't I ...." "Why did I ...." "Did I allow suffering to occur or to be prolonged?" "Why didn't I see ...." "If only ...." ad infinitum. I am always shocked at the issues that well up and threaten to swallow me whole. And the guilt never completely abates, no matter how many creatures I help through life and death. Each one is different from the rest, and each one's needs and desires are unique.

Such issues have tiny barbs that hook in and are tortuous to remove. But not one of them is necessary or healthy. So when I find guilt leering at me like a crowd of tiny gargoyles, I either sit down in the sunlight, or go for a long walk. Then I sit at my desk with paper and pen and review everything that nags at my brain or rips open my heart and demands justification.

Notice I stress *self*-judgment, because it is a personal job, not anyone else's. So at this stage of my healing I listen only to myself, never to friends, family members, or anyone else with advice, as well meaning as it might be. And when I've laid all my cards on the table, so-to-speak, I give myself exactly thirty minutes to sort them out. During this time I can berate myself, forgive myself, allow myself to be absolutely wretched and self-pitying. It is important to bring all those feelings up into the light.

After that, it's time to let them go. If, after thirty minutes I haven't completely resolved my guilt, I simply ask forgiveness of myself. Then, with as much calmness and clarity as possible, I turn within to my own center and ask for help and guidance. Even though I will make mistakes, I remind myself that I love all creatures. My reverence for the animal I have just helped, allowed me to act in the most appropriate way I knew, at the time. If I see things differently now, then I can also remember that I have, through such an experience, learned and grown.

Forgiving myself for what I feel I might have or have not done, is an essential first step toward any healing that needs to occur for myself. Animals, who love and forgive so completely and quickly, are excellent examples for me to follow.

The kindest, surest way to heal is with love, starting with myself. When I replenish myself with love, I can enter any new relationship with an animal without leftover reservations or guilt. If I hold onto the guilt, self-doubt will accompany me as I continue my work.

CELEBRATE THE ANIMAL'S NEW EXISTENCE

Death is a pause between stages of living, physical and nonphysical. I believe that after death, a being continues to be full of life, now in the form of spirit. These creature friends of ours really do love and appreciate us very much, their loyalty going beyond earthly obligation. While most of us are not clairvoyant enough to be aware of such a presence right after death, in quiet, unrelated moments, our animal companions may communicate with us, reassuring us that they are all right. Waggy's return a year following her death is a powerful example. And there have been others.

When my beagle, Parsley, disappeared one December day during hunting season, I mourned not only his absence, but the way he left the lives of myself and the family. If he had died at home I would have at least been assured he was not caged up somewhere, maybe being abused or neglected as hunting dogs can be. I worried that he might even be caught on a fence line up in the mountains, suffering a slow and painful death. Never coming home again meant any kind of resolution was on hold. There was always that tiny carrot of hope that Parsley might be found.

For a year I searched every lead. Weekly, I walked the rows of anxious, homeless faces at the local shelter. My grief and fear for Parsley rose to nearly unbearable levels. It was perhaps a test of my fortitude and faithfulness, yet despite the passage of time, the pain would not diminish.

One night, almost a year to the day Parsley disappeared, I had a dream in which I saw him running across a familiar hill, directly towards me. He was golden, radiant, his long hound ears flying out as he ran and his tail wagging joyfully. Everything about him exclaimed, "It's okay, I'm here on this side, see? I'm doing great!" After that dream, the mystery of Parsley's disappearance was resolved for me and I never went looking for him again.

Absolutely, I will always miss my beloved animal friends who have died. Yet, I also know there is a part of them still with me, the part I don't have to miss at all. I will continue to remember with joy all the wonderful things about them while they were alive. And, I will celebrate all they have now become in their new existence.

FIND AN UNDERSTANDING PERSON

Notice I don't write "sympathetic person" because I do not want sympathy at such a time. Someone who says, "Oh, you poor dear ...." does me no good whatsoever. I want support. Helpful words from a caring person might be, "Tell me about your friend; tell me how you feel; what was your experience like? Tell me ...." In other words, I need someone who is really interested in helping me bring to the surface all those feelings grinding away inside me, someone willing to *listen* and if appropriate, respond accordingly.

Sometimes all I need is another warm body to sit with me in silence, prayer, or meditation. Often, quiet support is the best. Many people are still very uncomfortable with death and/or honestly don't see any reason to get so worked up over an animal. To hear one's family or friends remark that such a special companion "was, after all, only a dog" (or whatever kind of creature he/she was) is exceedingly painful for the one grieving. However, there are grief groups, such as the Interspecies Support Team, that understand the profound sense of loss when an animal companion dies. This group of individuals is committed to compassionately helping others through such loss. These volunteers work from experience and understand the needs and feelings of others at such times. (See Resources.)

One night a woman called from California. We had never met, but her name was familiar to me. She was a long-standing subscriber to *laJoie*, the journal that I co-founded in 1990. She simply said, "Hello, is this Rita? This is Sandy ...." and before I could say much more than "Yes," she broke into uncontrolled sobbing. She managed to explain that her feline companion of many years was close to death. We talked quite awhile and at the conclusion of our conversation, she was much calmer. "Thank you," she said. "I just needed to talk to someone who would understand." A letter followed several weeks later in which she said that when her cat died, she was able to work through it all much better. So there really is no substitute for a supportive friend.

COMPLETING GOODBYES

Recently, I received a letter from a distraught woman whose cat had disappeared and several weeks later still had not returned. She feared coyotes had gotten him and as much as she mourned the loss of her cat, the fact that she had not had a chance to say goodbye was more painful. Her letter brought to my attention that this was also an issue for me with some of my animals who had died and I wasn't present. Surprisingly, once I allowed myself to explore my suppressed feelings, I realized this was a large unresolved issue in my own life that I needed to address.

As a result, I learned that it is never too late to say goodbye. The body may be gone, but the animal's spirit may still be very close to help us through our grieving. It's okay to keep on talking to that beloved creature until the need fades or disappears all together. Once my animal friends have died, it is healing for me to tell them, "I miss you! I miss your being with me, I miss your furry (feathered, shelled) self." Then

I add, "And I love you and am glad to know you are in such a fine place. Then I ask, always wondering, "Is it as fine as I think it must be, without a clumsy heavy body?"

You can always talk with your beloved companion, now a friend in spirit. If I can relax and allow free-flowing thoughts to enter my mind, surprising communications will come through to me, and quite possibly, through pencil or pen onto paper.

CREATE A TRIBUTE

Dear, ancient, Penny Partridge, that remarkable golden retriever who graced my life for six months, left a great gap in my heart when she died. Dr. Partridge had told me the difficult news that her cancer was inoperable and it was best to let her go. Of course, I agreed. But I spent most of the night drifting in and out of a restless sleep, as images and impressions of her wove through my dreams and semi-wakeful stupor. By morning, I was full of thoughts of her and I knew I had to write about her. What flowed was a long letter of appreciation to Dr. Partridge, his family, and staff. I told them what Penny had meant to me, how she had taught me important lessons, and blessed our time together with her enthusiastic and loving ways. When I finished the letter I knew it was the best tribute I could give to Penny Partridge, other than my pledge to continue helping older animals.

Writing is an essential means of expression for me, and so I usually create a tribute after one of my companions has moved on. Usually I write an essay, or a poem. But a tribute, no matter what its form, is something that, by its very existence is joyous, and helps completion. Sometimes I make something with my hands, allowing my intuitive right brain to create a memorial that will bring me, and hopefully others, pleasure and insight. Whatever the form, I know I am giving birth to a portion of that creature's true nature all over again.

One of the most successful tributes in terms of helping myself and others is the designing, planting, and tending of a prayer garden.

While I started these a few years ago out of a strong inner urge, some information received from an elderly neighbor proved intriguing.

It seems that the original house and property we now own once belonged to a woman fondly known as Miss Mattie. I know nothing else about the former owner except that while she lived here, she planted what she called "prayer gardens" throughout the property. When we bought the place, all trace of the gardens were gone — only lawn, woods, and a vegetable garden remained. While I grew up with a grandmother and mother who both loved gardens and nurtured that love in both my sister and me, I began my flower and herb gardens at my sanctuary almost as if I was being gently guided to do so. I began to create small gardens in memory of certain people and animals who had either died, or were doing special work for Earth. I guess I was subconsciously re-creating Ms. Mattie's prayer gardens.

A prayer garden is a grand tribute. Turning the soil, selecting plants, and tending to them is nurturing to me. In our family, we have so many creatures who come in and go out of our sanctuary, I am turning the entire front lawn into gardens of various sizes and shapes, with a small pond, a Japanese Zen rock garden of white stone, and a variety of exotic trees. In the center is a circle garden that faces the rising sun and the ring of magnificent Blue Ridge Mountains. When people pass by on the road they can also see the gardens and their beauty as well. A stone statue of St. Francis holding a bird welcomes visitors, and nearby, a blue-terracotta bird bath serves the birds during the warm months. The gardens bloom with marigolds, lobelia, and pansies interspersed with daisies of all varieties, purple echinacea, geraniums, hollyhocks, and herbs. Several wild plants have volunteered to join the garden: dandelions, buttercups, violets, and purple, white and yellow clover. Each year new plants are added and the gardens are extended with paths and rocks and trees.

A garden tribute doesn't need to be so elaborate or large as the one I have just described. It could become a lot of hard work to maintain and then it defeats its own purpose. Sometimes, especially in late summer,

I look at the weeds that invariably get ahead of me and wonder what I have gotten myself into! But maybe it's Ms. Mattie's spirit, or my intense love of flowers and animals that will not let me give up.

When I take a moment from daily chores to sit in the grass by the gardens, weeds and all, and look across the fields to the mountains, I am reminded of the camaraderie of all life, wild and domesticated, that includes me. I consider with gratitude all those who have come to stay here for the span of their lives, those who are now present with me, and those yet to arrive. Gardens, and more specifically nature, are a wonderful reflection of the perfection inherent in such impermanence: the seasons, the life cycle of annuals and perennials, the flow of clouds, the constantly changing weather patterns, and of course, all that is life and death.

Gardens are not always possible for everyone, in which case I suggest planting a tree, perhaps a flowering one, or a shrub. Even keeping a potted plant can be a wonderful tribute. There are other ways to honor another, among them assembling a scrapbook of photographs and thoughts about that animal companion, or giving a donation to a favorite organization in his or her name.

Most importantly, I encourage everyone to understand that forgetting an animal companion is not necessary, and hardly possible in my experience. Nor should grief be denied or suppressed. I am not afraid to cry, sometimes long and hard. When I cry the pain becomes its own cleanser. And while I do limit my guilt, I allow grief its reasonable time, whether that takes one day or years.

Healing comes as it always does, bit by bit, much as a brilliant dawn overtaking night. During the healing I keep talking out loud to the soul of my friend, letting her or him know precisely how I feel, how much I wish them well, that I will be just fine, and how great it will be to know them again. Which side of life will we next meet on, spirit or physical? Who knows? I do know we will once again join forces with all that love holding us close. How could we do otherwise? How could such a strong and sacred bond ever be broken? It is a thought that always comforts me.

The little furry face, the eyes, the voice, the warm body, the idiosyncrasies that make each creature unique, the trust and loyalty, and the sharing of joy and pain — these are all things I hold onto. These are all treasures for me, left by a very dear friend who graced my life, and always will.

So I am left with something after all! Not just the guilt and pain; not just the empty spot, the old food bowl, the unused bed; not just the stuff about destiny and fate and is-there-life-after death syndrome. I'm left with all these neat memories I can sort through, keep close, and enjoy for a very long time.

⌐

When I hold a dying creature either in my arms or in my mind, I feel a merging of greater purpose that springs from Spirit, which is our true nature. When I do this, I believe it is the quintessence of compassion — the giving over of oneself directly into the needs, the calling out for help from another. It is the equivalent of being an angelic presence in human form, just as my animal friend is angel in animal form.

Once a connection of souls is consciously made, the link is eternal and unlimited. I am sure we will meet again. A bond of love always forms a thread between us and our animal companions that can never be broken.

Sorrow and grief will wend their way into the process of dying and I accept that. These emotions are part of the sacred process of mystical expansion that carry me into expansive experiences of love.

To continue my daily work with elderly, sick, and dying animals, I have to accept my own feelings of sadness and loss and then release myself from doubts about life beyond the death of the body. Then I can continue to be loving and gentle, ready to accept whatever new animals await me.

With great assuredness, I believe that as we approach the bridge of transition together, our angelic beings of light are there to assist each of us. My animal friend must release ties to Earth, and I must release my grief. At the crest of that bridge we embrace one another, wish each other well, and pledge to meet again. I trust that *we* are the Shared Heart — inseparable, eternal, perfect.

FIFTEEN

It's Really All Right:
A Final Tribute

Arthur never complained. Although he was obviously gravely ill, he studied us with dark, almond-shaped eyes, riding the intense waves of pain as only a rabbit can, with dignity, silence, and acceptance. Later that afternoon, he died in surgery. As with all the animals who have graced our sanctuary, Arthur left us with a gift of love. And that love, like a pebble tossed into a forest pond, moved outward to embrace all who had known him.

There was no need to mourn, but I did, staring at the carefully taped box in my hands and wondering, "Why?"

"But we know why," Tim, just turned twelve, reminded me. "Wasn't it his time to go?"

"Yes," I said, sniffling.

"Then it's really all right that he died," he replied as he placed the large russet rabbit in his grave beneath the sunflowers.

"He was brave," fourteen-year-old Michael noted.

"And everybody loved him," Tim added.

As the brothers knelt side by side, patting the freshly dug earth over their friend, Michael added, "And he loved everyone back."

"And he really isn't gone," Tim declared brightly.

Michael looked sharply at his younger brother. Then Tim pointed to the new rabbit pen behind them where seven tiny, eager bunnies peered curiously at the children. "There's half of Arthur in all of them," Tim noted.

"Yeah," Michael said, sighing softly, almost with a smile.

For awhile, we sat back on the garden path, wiping our tears and chewing mint leaves.

"Arthur would like this funeral," Michael said.

Tim spit out a stem. "Think where he's at they have mint?"

"Sure do," I said. "Would God forget the mint?"

And the more we discussed rabbits and God, the more we felt the sacred presence throughout the garden. It was as if a spirit of bright remembrance danced about the flower beds that once had been Arthur's home. Our fragile hearts began to fill, not with longing and grief, but thoughtfulness and joy.

"I can feel Spirit everywhere and in everything," I remarked.

"So Arthur had a spirit?" Michael asked.

"Sure, dummy," Tim interrupted, throwing a piece of pine bark at his brother. "There's Spirit in rabbits and us and Mom and the mint ...."

Michael laid aside the sprig in his hand, wrinkling up his nose. "You mean I've been chewing on Spirit?"

"No," I replied. "Spirit is universal energy, light, and love. That energy in the mint is simply joining that same energy in you."

Despite my explanation, Michael lay the fragrant stalk of leaves on the small grave.

"Arthur reflected that energy more so than most other rabbits," I added. My children looked up at me questioningly. Always in our frequent discussions in the past we had considered all life as equally wonderful. Now I was confusing them by placing one rabbit above the others.

"Do you remember," I continued, "that Dr. Partridge said there was something special about this particular rabbit?" The boys nodded their heads. "And remember how everyone came to see him and how they wanted to hold him?"

"Sure," Tim broke in, " 'cause he was so beautiful and friendly."

"Exactly," I said. "And what about Henrietta?"

"What about her?" Tim flashed back defensively, looking over at his little black-and-white Dutch rabbit in her pen.

"She's beautiful too, but …."

"She growls and scratches if you get too close," Michael interrupted.

"And nobody wants to hold her," Tim admitted.

"So what made Arthur *extra* beautiful?" I asked.

Michael looked up through wet eyes. "He was gentle and friendly and liked everyone who talked to him."

"He was easy and pleasant to be around," I said, watching the boys' faces.

"You mean," Michael said, looking steadily back now, "easy to love."

"Yes," I said.

We stood up and moved to form a circle around the grave. We joined hands and whispered a prayer, sending our love and gratitude outward into the garden. And that love flowed past the flower beds, past the mint patch, past the mountains to whatever dimension in which Arthur now resided.

"It really pays off to be friendly," Tim remarked quietly.

"Yes," I agreed. "It's sort of like sharing. When you give love, it keeps coming right back around to you, but in greater and greater amounts."

"Like all the people we know who loved Arthur so much," Michael added.

"Right," I replied, feeling that peace and acceptance I had come to know from Arthur flooding through me. "And Arthur's probably very happy now, tucked away in a celestial bed of mint and having a great time."

"And spreading love around," Tim added.

Michael turned toward the house, stooped to pick one more piece of mint, then looked back at Arthur's bright and bounding offspring crowding around Tim for his affection.

"Yeah, for once, Tim, I have to agree with you," he said softly, a smile poking tentatively at his cheeks. "I really think everything is all right."

Resources

GRIEVING AND LOSS

Forever Friends, Resolving Grief After the Loss of a Beloved Animal
by Joan Coleman

Goodbye, Friend: Healing Wisdom for Anyone Who Has Ever Lost a Pet
by Gary Kowalski

Healing the Pain of Pet Loss, Letters in Memoriam
edited by Kymberly Smith

Journey Through Pet Loss — Revised Edition 2000
by Deborah Antinori, two-tape audio set
Website: www.petlossaudio.com or 800-431-1579

Pet Loss: A Spiritual Guide by Eleanor L. Harris

Pet Loss, A Thoughtful Guide for Adults and Children
by Herbert A. Nieburg, Ph.D. and Arlene Fischer

The Loss of a Pet by Wallace Sife, Ph.D.

Three Cats, Two Dogs, One Journey Through Multiple Pet Loss
by David Congalton. Website: www.davidcongalton.com

*When Your Pet Outlives You: Protecting Animal Companions
After You Die*
by David Congalton and Charlotte Alexander *(available May 2002)*

CONSCIOUS DYING WORK

Healing Into Life and Death by Stephen Levine

*Meetings at the Edge: Dialogues with the Grieving and the Dying, the
Healing and the Healed* by Stephen Levine

Who Dies? An Investigation of Conscious Living and Conscious Dying
by Stephen Levine

SPIRITUALITY AND ANIMALS' SOULS

Animals as Guides for the Soul by Susan Chernak McElroy

Animals as Teachers and Healers: True Stories and Reflections
by Susan Chernak McElroy

Ishmael by Daniel Quinn

Journey Into Nature, A Spiritual Adventure by Michael J. Roads

Life, Hope & Healing, Prescriptions from the Heart
by Bernie S. Siegel, M.D., six-tape audio set

A Snowflake in My Hand by Samantha Mooney

The Soul of Your Pet: Evidence for the Survival of Animals in the Afterlife by Scott S. Smith

The Souls of Animals by Gary Kowalski

When Elephants Weep: The Emotional Lives of Animals by Jeffrey Moussaieff Masson and Susan McCarthy

ANIMAL COMMUNICATION

Animal Talk: Interspecies Telepathic Communication by Penelope Smith

Animal Wisdom, Communications with Animals by Anita Curtis

Conversations with Animals: Cherished Messages and Memories as Told by an Animal Communicator by Lydia Hiby with Bonnie Weintraub

Dolphin Dreamtime, The Art and Science of Interspecies Communication by Jim Nollman

How to Hear the Animals by Anita Curtis, book and tape set Available from Anita Curtis, listed page 159.

Spoken In Whispers, The Autobiography of a Horse Whisperer by Nicci MacKay

HEALING

Bach Flower Remedies for Animals
by Stefan Ball and Judy Howard Flower

Chanting: Discovering Spirit in Sound
by Robert Gass with Kathleen Brehony

Colour, Twelve Lectures by Rudolf Steiner

Flower Essences, Reordering Our Understanding and Approach to Illness and Health by Machaelle Small Wright

Healing and Regeneration Through Color/Music by Corinne Heline

Music as Medicine: The Art and Science of Healing with Sound by Kay Gardner, six-tape audio set. Available from Sounds True, listed page 158.

On Wings of Song, music by Robert Gass. Available from Spring Hill Music, listed page 158.

Perelandra Essences Guide by Machaelle S. Wright. Available from The Perelandra Flower Essences, listed page 158.

The Power of Prayer: Connecting with the Wisdom of the Universe by Larry Dossey, M.D., six-tape set

Why Is Cancer Killing Our Pets? How You Can Protect and Treat Your Animal Companion by Deborah Straw

CHILDREN'S BOOKS

Cat Heaven and *Dog Heaven* by Cynthia Rylant

The Fall of Freddie the Leaf: A Story of Life for All Ages by Leo F. Buscaglia, Ph.D.

I'll Always Love You by Hans Wilhelm

The Tenth Good Thing About Barney by Judith Viorst and Erik Blegvad

MINDFULNESS MEDITATION, CENTERING, ENERGY WORK

Bringing the Mind Home by Sogyal Rinpoche, audio tape

The Dancing Wu Li Masters: An Overview of the New Physics by Gary Zukav and David Finkelstein

A Gradual Awakening by Stephen Levine

Hands of Light: A Guide to Healing Through the Human Energy Field by Barbara Ann Brennan

The Heart of Understanding, Commentaries on the Prajnaparamita Heart Sutra by Thich Nhat Hanh and Peter Levitt

Light Emerging: The Journey of Personal Healing by Barbara Ann Brennan and Thomas J. Schneider

LovingKindness Meditation: Learning to Love Through Insight Meditation by Sharon Salzberg, two-set audio tape

A New Vision of Living and Dying by Sogyal Rinpoche, audio tape

Peace is Every Step, the Path of Mindfulness in Everyday Life by Thich Nhat Hanh

Still Here: Embracing Aging, Changing, and Dying by Ram Dass

The Tibetan Book of Living and Dying by Sogyal Rinpoche

Wherever You Go There You Are: Mindfulness Meditation in Everyday Life by Jon Kabat-Zin

PUBLICATIONS

laJoie, The Journal That Honors All Beings. Quarterly publication, Rita M. Reynolds, Mary K. Birkholz, editors. For a sample issue, information, or to submit manuscripts, contact laJoie and Company, PO Box 145, Batesville, VA 22924; email: lajoieco1@aol.com; website: www.Lajoieandco1@aol.com

The Latham Letter published by The Latham Foundation for the Promotion of Humane Education. For information contact 1826 Clement & Schiller Streets, Alameda, CA 94501; 510-521-9861; email: Latham@aol.com; website: www.latham.org

TOOLS FOR HEALING

Anaflora Flower Essences. Contact Sharon Callahan, PO Box 1056, Mount Shasta, CA 96067; email: anaflora@snowcrest.com; website: www.anaflora.com

The Dr. Edward Bach Center. Mount Vernon, Sotwell, Oxfordshire. 0X10 0PZ England; email: mail@bachcentre.com; website: www.bachcentre.com

Interspecies Support Team: Helping Animals and the People Who Care for Them. For information and a list of volunteers, please send a self-addressed stamped business size envelope to laJoie and Company, PO Box 145, Batesville, VA 22924, email: lajoieco1@aol.com

Herbal Peak Herbals. Respectfully grown, harvested, and prepared herbal tinctures, salves, and oils for humans and animals by Bill and Tina Hodge. Catalog available: PO Box 6, Eagleville, CA 96110; 530-279-2184

The Perelandra Flower Essences. Contact PO Box 3603, Warrenton, VA 22186; 540-937-2153.

Sounds True. Produces wonderful audio tapes. Catalog available: PO Box 8010, Boulder, CO, 80306; 800-333-9185.

Spring Hill Music. For a catalog, which includes Robert Gass's music, contact PO Box 800, Boulder, CO 80306.

Warm Rock Tapes. Offers guided meditations and talks by Stephen Levine. Contact Warm Rock Tapes, PO Box 108, Chamisal, NM 87521.

ANIMAL COMMUNICATORS

I highly recommend the following communicators. Contact directly for appointments and fees.

Sharon Callahan, Anaflora, Box 1056, Mount Shasta, CA 96067 Email: anaflora@snowcrest.com; web site: www.anaflora.com

Anita Curtis, P.O. Box 182, Gilbertsville, PA 19525-0182. Email: amicom@aol.com

Lydia Hiby, 10932 Arleta Ave., Mission Hills, CA. 818-365-4647; web site: www.lydiahiby.com

Gigi Kast, 61 Harrington Road, Walpole, ME 04573. 207-677-2190. Email: shanoagi@lincoln.midcoast.com

Kate Reilly, 321 Orangeburg Street S.E., Aiken, SC 29801. 803-644-6666.

About the Author

Rita Reynolds is the founder of Howling Success, an animal sanctuary located in the foothills of the Blue Ridge Mountains near Charlottesville, Virginia. For the past twenty-five years her sanctuary has been home to hundreds of animals. Reynolds is also the founder and editor of *laJoie, The Journal in Appreciation of All Animals,* first published in 1990 and distributed internationally. Reynolds is currently establishing a community hospice program for animals and their human families. In addition to her animal family, Reynolds and her husband have two grown sons.

If you are interested in animal hospice work or would like to help set-up an animal hospice program, please contact Rita Reynolds. Also, she is collecting unusual or inspiring stories about experiences with animals related to animal death and dying, after-death communication, and after-death encounters. Reynolds would like to consider your story for inclusion in a future book project. Contact her at: PO Box 145, Batesville, VA 22924. She can also be reached by email at: Lajoieco1@aol.com or visit her web site at: www.lajoiemag.com.

Other Titles by NewSage Press

NewSage Press has published several titles related to animals. We hope these books will inspire humanity towards a more compassionate and respectful treatment of all living beings.

Three Cats, Two Dogs, One Journey Through Multiple Pet Loss
by David Congalton

When Your Pet Outlives You: Protecting Animal Companions After You Die
by David Congalton and Charlotte Alexander *(available May 2002)*

Conversations with Animals: Cherished Messages and Memories as Told by an Animal Communicator
by Lydia Hiby with Bonnie Weintraub

Food Pets Die For: Shocking Facts About Pet Food
by Ann N. Martin

Protect Your Pet: More Shocking Facts
by Ann N. Martin

Unforgettable Mutts: Pure of Heart Not of Breed
by Karen Derrico

Singing to the Sound: Visions of Nature, Animals & Spirit
by Brenda Peterson

Dancer on the Grass: True Stories About Horses and People
by Teresa Tsimmu Martino

The Wolf, the Woman, the Wilderness: A True Story of Returning Home
by Teresa Tsimmu Martino

NEWSAGE PRESS

For more information visit our web site
www.newsagepress.com
or request a catalog from NewSage Press
PO Box 607, Troutdale, OR 97060-0607
Phone Toll Free 877-695-2211, Fax 503-695-5406
Email: info@newsagepress.com
Distributed to bookstores by Publishers Group West
800-788-3123(U.S.) or 416-934-9900 (Canada)